LEVEL 7

ULTIMATE MUSIC THEORY

By Glory St. Germain ARCT RMT MYCC UMTC &
Shelagh McKibbon-U'Ren RMT UMTC

The LEVEL 7 Supplemental Workbook is designed to be completed after the Intermediate Rudiments and LEVEL 6 Supplemental Workbooks.

GSG MUSIC

Enriching Lives Through Music Education

ISBN: 978-1-927641-58-3

The Ultimate Music Theory™ Program

The Ultimate Music Theory™ Program lays the foundation of music theory education.

The focus of the Ultimate Music Theory Program is to simplify complex concepts and show the relativity of these concepts with practical application. This program is designed to help teachers and students discover the excitement and benefits of a sound music theory education.

The Ultimate Music Theory Program is based on a proven approach to the study of music theory that follows the *"must have"* Learning Principles to develop effective learning for all learning styles.

The Ultimate Music Theory™ Program and Supplemental Workbooks help students prepare for nationally recognized theory examinations including the Royal Conservatory of Music.

GSG MUSIC — gloryland PUBLISHING

Library and Archives Canada Cataloguing in Publication
UMT Supplemental Series / Glory St. Germain and Shelagh McKibbon-U'Ren

Gloryland Publishing - UMT Supplemental Workbook and Answer Book Series:

GP-SPL	ISBN: 978-1-927641-41-5	UMT Supplemental Prep Level
GP-SL1	ISBN: 978-1-927641-42-2	UMT Supplemental Level 1
GP-SL2	ISBN: 978-1-927641-43-9	UMT Supplemental Level 2
GP-SL3	ISBN: 978-1-927641-44-6	UMT Supplemental Level 3
GP-SL4	ISBN: 978-1-927641-45-3	UMT Supplemental Level 4
GP-SL5	ISBN: 978-1-927641-46-0	UMT Supplemental Level 5
GP-SL6	ISBN: 978-1-927641-47-7	UMT Supplemental Level 6
GP-SL7	ISBN: 978-1-927641-48-4	UMT Supplemental Level 7
GP-SL8	ISBN: 978-1-927641-49-1	UMT Supplemental Level 8
GP-SCL	ISBN: 978-1-927641-50-7	UMT Supplemental Complete Level
GP-SPLA	ISBN: 978-1-927641-51-4	UMT Supplemental Prep Level Answer Book
GP-SL1A	ISBN: 978-1-927641-52-1	UMT Supplemental Level 1 Answer Book
GP-SL2A	ISBN: 978-1-927641-53-8	UMT Supplemental Level 2 Answer Book
GP-SL3A	ISBN: 978-1-927641-54-5	UMT Supplemental Level 3 Answer Book
GP-SL4A	ISBN: 978-1-927641-55-2	UMT Supplemental Level 4 Answer Book
GP-SL5A	ISBN: 978-1-927641-56-9	UMT Supplemental Level 5 Answer Book
GP-SL6A	ISBN: 978-1-927641-57-6	UMT Supplemental Level 6 Answer Book
GP-SL7A	ISBN: 978-1-927641-58-3	UMT Supplemental Level 7 Answer Book
GP-SL8A	ISBN: 978-1-927641-59-0	UMT Supplemental Level 8 Answer Book
GP-SCLA	ISBN: 978-1-927641-60-6	UMT Supplemental Complete Level Answer Book

Respect Copyright - Copyright 2017 Gloryland Publishing

All rights reserved. No part of this publication may be reproduced or transmitted in any form or by any means, electronic or mechanical, including photocopying, recording, or any information storage and retrieval system, without permission in writing from the author/publisher.

* Resources - An annotated list is available at UltimateMusicTheory.com under Free Resources.

Ultimate Music Theory
LEVEL 7 Supplemental
Table of Contents

Ultimate Music Theory	The Story of UMT… Meet So-La & Ti-Do …………..………………..	4
Comparison Chart	Level 7 ……………………………………………..…………………	6
Note/Rest Review	Dotted, Double Dotted Notes/Rests, Irregular Groups …………….	8
Scales Review	Enharmonic, Whole Tone, Octatonic, Pentatonic, Blues …………..	12
Interval Review	Aug, Per, Maj, min, dim, Inversions & Enharmonic Equivalent …….	20
Transposition	Intervals of Transposition & Accidentals …..………..…………….	24
Triad Type/Quality	Root/Quality Chord Symbols, Functional Chord Symbols ………….	28
Chord Positions	Dominant Seventh Chords, Inversions & Accidentals ………………	32
Dominant 7th Chords	Writing Chords & Inversions - Key Signature ………………………..	36
Diminished 7th Chords	Leading-Tone Diminished Seventh Chords ……..………………….	38
Open/Close Position	Major/minor triads, Dom 7th & dim 7th chords, SATB Texture …….	40
Cadence Identification	Authentic Cadence & Half Cadence ………………………………..	42
Writing Cadences	Keyboard Style Cadences at Phrase Endings …………….……….	46
Terms and Analysis	Performance Terms & Italian Terms ……………………….....…….	48
Melody Analysis	Non-chord tones & Functional Chord Symbols ……………………..	50
Melody Writing	Melodic Decoration - Tones & Non-Chord Tones …………………..	52
Composing	Contrasting Period and Consequent Phrases ………………………	54
Contrasting Period	Melodic Structure and Rhythmic Structure ………………………..	56
Form & Analysis	Harmonic Progressions and Harmonic Rhythm ………..………….	58
Melody Writing	Imagine, Compose, Explore & Sight Reading - Forest Frog ……….	60
Romantic Era	Mendelssohn, Overture to a Midsummer Night's Dream ………….	62
Frédéric Chopin	Chopin, *Étude* Op. 10, No. 12 (*Revolutionary Étude*) ……………..	66
Modern Era	Stravinsky, Petrushka (Ballet) ………………………………………..	70
Hugh Le Caine	Le Caine, Dripsody (Étude for Variable Speed Recorder) …………	74
Duke Ellington	Edward Kennedy "Duke" Ellington, Ko-Ko …………………………..	72
Music History Review	Baroque, Classical, Romantic & Modern …………………………..	78
Dom 7th & Dim 7th	Game - Name That 7th ………………………………………………..	80
Theory Exam	Level 7 ……………………………………….......…………………….	81
Certificate	Completion of Level 7 …………………….......…………………….	88

Score: 60 - 69 Pass; 70 - 79 Honors; 80 - 89 First Class Honors; 90 - 100 First Class Honors with Distinction

Ultimate Music Theory: *The Way to Score Success!*

Ultimate Music Theory
The Story of UMT…

Once upon a time there were two music teachers, Glory St. Germain and Shelagh McKibbon-U'Ren, who were passionate about enriching lives through music education!

Their friendship, their desire to inspire teachers and to help students master musicianship skills is evident in the Ultimate Music Theory Program & Certification Course.

Glory (author of the Ultimate Music Theory Series) and Shelagh (author of the UMT Exam Series) are dedicated to helping students of all learning styles and abilities.

Glory St. Germain & Shelagh McKibbon-U'Ren

Their creative genius is presented here in the Ultimate Music Theory Supplemental Workbook Series.

Glory St. Germain ARCT RMT MYCC UMTC is the Founder/CEO of GSG MUSIC. Glory is a Royal Conservatory of Music Certified Teacher, Neuro-Linguistic Practitioner and sought-after clinician. She served as President - MRMTA, CC - MusicLink & MB Coordinator for Music for Young Children.

Shelagh McKibbon-U'Ren RMT UMTC is the Examiner/Editor of the UMT Program & Online Courses. Shelagh, a member of ORMTA, teaches piano, theory, voice, harmony and history. Special training in working with emotional and behavioral needs children brings massive success to her teaching.

These Ultimate Music Theory Certified Teachers are acknowledged for their contributions.

Ruth Douglas ARCT (in Teaching and in Piano Performance) RMT UMTC B.Sc. B.Ed. UMT Harmony, History and Analysis Consultant Ruth Douglas teaches piano and theory, preparing students for examinations with both the RCM and Conservatory Canada. Ruth has a lifelong passion for learning, for sharing knowledge and for helping others to be the best that they can be.

Julianne Warkentin ARCT RMT UMTC. Ultimate Piano Series Composer Julianne Warkentin is an award winning piano, composition & theory teacher. Her dedication to educating teachers and students about composition, analysis and performance encourages musicians of all ages to imagine, compose and explore the magic of music.

Joanne Barker UMTC. Ultimate Music Theory Games Creator Joanne Barker is an experienced piano/theory teacher and detail-oriented creative designer. Her expertise and knowledge of teaching music theory with inventive and out-of-the-box ideas brings excellence to the creation of the UMT Games.

ULTIMATE MUSIC THEORY

At Ultimate Music Theory we are passionate about helping teachers and students experience the joy of teaching and learning music by creating the most effective music theory materials on the planet!

Introducing the Ultimate Music Theory Family!

So-La

Ti-Do

Meet So-La! So-La loves to sing and dance.

She is expressive, creative and loves to tell stories through music!

So-La feels music in her heart. She loves to teach, compose and perform.

Meet Ti-Do! Ti-Do loves to count and march.

He is rhythmic, consistent and loves the rules of music theory!

Ti-Do feels music in his hands and feet. He loves to analyze, share tips and conduct.

So-La & Ti-Do will guide you through Mastering Music Theory!

Enriching Lives Through Music Education

The Ultimate Music Theory™ Comparison Chart to the 2016 Royal Conservatory of Music Theory Syllabus.
Level 7

The Ultimate Music Theory™ Rudiments Workbooks, Supplemental Workbooks and Exams prepare students for successful completion of the Royal Conservatory of Music Theory Levels.

UMT Intermediate Rudiments Workbook plus the LEVEL 6 Supplemental Workbook = RCM Theory Level 6.
♫ Note: Additional completion of the LEVEL 7 Supplemental Workbook = RCM Theory Level 7.

RCM Level 7 Theory Concept	Ultimate Music Theory Intermediate Workbook
Required Keys - Major and minor keys up to seven sharps and flats	**Keys Covered** - Major and minor keys up to seven sharps and flats
Pitch and Notation - Transposition of melodies up or down by any interval or to any key	**Pitch and Notation Covered** - Transposition of melodies in Major keys up by any interval within an octave * Workbook Pages - Transposition up or down; Major to Major; minor to minor
Scales and Scale Degree Names - Chromatic, whole-tone and octatonic scales starting on any pitch (using key signatures or accidentals) - Major and minor pentatonic scales, starting on any pitch (using key signatures or accidentals) - Blues scales, starting on any pitch (using key signatures and/or accidentals)	**Scales and Scale Degree Names Covered** - Chromatic scales (Harmonic & Melodic), Whole Tone and Octatonic scales starting on any pitch (using Key Signatures or Accidentals) - Major and minor Pentatonic scales, starting on any pitch (using Key Signatures or Accidentals) - Blues scales, starting on any pitch (using Key Signature and/or Accidentals) * Workbook Pages - Scale Review - Writing Scales based on hints * Workbook Pages - Review - 20th Century Scales
Rhythm and Meter - Double dotted notes and rests - Irregular groupings (duplets, triplets, quadruplets, quintuplets, sextuplets and septuplets) - Application of time signatures, bar lines and rests	**Rhythm and Meter Covered** * Workbook Page - Review - Double Dotted Notes * Workbook Page - Understanding Double Dotted Rest Values ~ not used in standard rhythm and meter at this level ~ - Irregular Groups in Simple & Compound Time (all required groupings) * Workbook Page - Review - Irregular Group - Application of Time Signatures, Bar Lines and rests in Simple and Compound Time
Intervals - All Intervals and their inversions within an octave, including enharmonic equivalents (using key signatures or accidentals) - Enharmonic Equivalent Intervals	**Intervals Covered** - All Intervals and their inversions (Major, minor, Perfect, Augmented, diminished) within an octave, above and below a given note (using Key Signatures or Accidentals) - writing and identifying intervals * Workbook Pages - Review - Enharmonic Equivalent Intervals * Workbook Pages - Review - Writing and Identifying Intervals * Workbook Page - Review - Inversions of Intervals
Form and Analysis - Identification of concepts from this and previous levels within short music examples - Application of Functional or Root/Quality Chord Symbols to a melody, using root-position I, IV and V chords (Major keys) or i, iv and V (minor keys), maintaining a harmonic rhythm of one chord measure	**Form and Analysis Covered** * Workbook Pages - Identification of concepts from this and previous levels within short music examples * Workbook Pages - Application of Functional Chord Symbols and Root/Quality Chord Symbols of a melody, using Root Position and Inversions (Major: I, IV and V; minor: i, iv and V) maintaining a harmonic rhythm of one chord per measure.

RCM Level 7 Theory Concept (Continued)

Chords and Harmony

- Diminished and augmented triads, in root position and inversions
- Triads built on any degree of a Major or minor (harmonic) scale using Functional Chord Symbols and Root/Quality Chord Symbols
- Leading-tone diminished 7th chords in minor keys, root position only, using Functional Chord Symbols and Root/Quality Chord Symbols
- Dominant 7th chords and their inversions, using Functional Chord Symbols and Root/Quality Chord Symbols
- Identification and writing of authentic and half cadences on a grand staff, using root-position chords in Major and minor keys, in keyboard style

Musical Terms and Signs

- Tempo, Dynamics and Articulation

Melody and Composition

- Melodic passing and neighbor tones (unaccented only), within a harmonic context of I, IV and V (Major keys) or i, iv and V (minor keys)
- Composition of a contrasting period in a major key, given the antecedent phrase

Music History/Appreciation

Guided Listening: "Overture to a Midsummer Night's Dream" by Felix Mendelssohn. Listening Focus: Program music and concert overture

Guided Listening: "Etude in c minor, op. 10, no. 12 ("Revolutionary")" by Frederic Chopin. Listening Focus: Etude, nationalism and chromatic harmony

Guided Listening: "Petrushka" - First Tableau: "The Crowd Revels at the Shrovetide Fair" by Igor Stravinsky. Listening Focus: Ballet, polytonality, rondo form and pentatonic scale

Guided Listening: "Dripsody" by Hugh LeCaine. Listening Focus: Electronic music

Guided Listening: "Ko-Ko" by Duke Ellington. Listening Focus: Jazz, twelve-bar blues

Examination

Level 7 Theory Examination

Ultimate Music Theory Intermediate Workbook (Continued)

Chords and Harmony Covered

* Workbook Pages - Diminished and Augmented Triads, in Root Position and Inversions
* Workbook Pages - Triads Built on Major Scales
* Workbook Pages - Triads Built on Minor Harmonic Scales (Including Functional Chord Symbols and Root/Quality Chord Symbols)
* Workbook Pages - Leading-Tone Diminished 7th Chords in minor keys, root position only, using Functional Chord Symbols and Root/Quality Chord Symbols
* Workbook Pages - Dominant 7th Chords and their inversions, using Functional Chord Symbols and Root/Quality Chord Symbols

- Identification of Authentic (Perfect), Half (Imperfect) and Plagal Cadences on a Grand Staff in Keyboard Style
* Workbook Pages - Writing Authentic and Half Cadences on a Grand Staff in Keyboard Style

Musical Terms and Signs Covered

* Workbook Pages - Musical Terms and Signs
* Workbook Page Bonus - Analysis and Sight Reading

Melody and Composition Covered

* Workbook Pages - Unaccented Passing Tones and Unaccented Neighbor Tones within a harmonic context of I, IV and V (Major keys) or i, iv and V (minor keys)
* Workbook Pages - Composition of a Contrasting Period (Major Key), given the Antecedent Phrase

Music History/Appreciation Covered

* Workbook Pages - Life and Music of Felix Mendelssohn; "Overture to a Midsummer Night's Dream" by Felix Mendelssohn. Listening Focus: Program Music and Concert Overture
Free Resources for Listening Activities & Watching Videos

* Workbook Pages - Life and Music of Frederic Chopin; "Etude in c minor, Opus 10, No. 12 ("Revolutionary")", by Frederic Chopin. Listening Focus: Etude, Nationalism and Chromatic Harmony
Free Resources for Listening Activities & Watching Videos

* Workbook Pages - Life and Music of Igor Stravinsky; "Petrushka" - First Tableau: "The Crowd Revels at the Shrovetide Fair" by Igor Stravinsky. Listening Focus: Ballet, Polytonality, Rondo Form and Pentatonic Scale
Free Resources for Listening Activities & Watching Videos

* Workbook Pages - "Dripsody" by Hugh LeCaine. Listening Focus: Electronic music
Free Resources for Listening Activities & Watching Videos

* Workbook Pages - "Ko-Ko" by Duke Ellington. Listening Focus: Jazz and Twelve-Bar Blues
Free Resources for Listening Activities & Watching Videos

Review Tests & Final Exam

- 12 Accumulative Review Tests (1 with each of the 12 Lessons)
* UMT Level 7 Theory Exam
* UMT Exam Series - Intermediate Rudiments

Get your **UltimateMusicTheoryApp.com** - Over 7000 Flashcards including audio! Learn Faster with all 6 Subjects: Beginner - Prep, Basic, Intermediate, Advanced, Ear Training & Music Trivia (including History).

NOTE VALUE REVIEW - INCLUDING DOTTED NOTES and DOUBLE DOTTED NOTES

Dotted Notes: A dot adds half the value of the note.

Double Dotted Notes: The first dot adds half the value of the note; the second dot adds half the value of the first dot.

So-La Says: While not common, double dotted notes have been used to add drama to rhythm.

First Dot = adds half the value of the note; plus
Second Dot = adds half the value of the first dot.

Double Dotted Breve note:

Double Dotted Whole note:

Double Dotted Half note:

Double Dotted Quarter note:

Double Dotted Eighth note:

Double Dotted Sixteenth note:

Double Dotted Notes can be found in several Beethoven Sonatas, including the Scherzo from his Sonata No. 18 in E-flat Major.

♫ **Ti-Do Tip:** Review "Music, Math and Dotted Notes" in the LEVEL 6 Supplemental Workbook (page 10).

1. Write one double dotted note that equals the total value of the notes when added together (combined).

2. For the following melodic excerpt from Beethoven's Sonata Opus 10, No. 1, Adagio molto, follow the example (at "A") and analyze the dotted and double dotted notes by writing out the single note values.

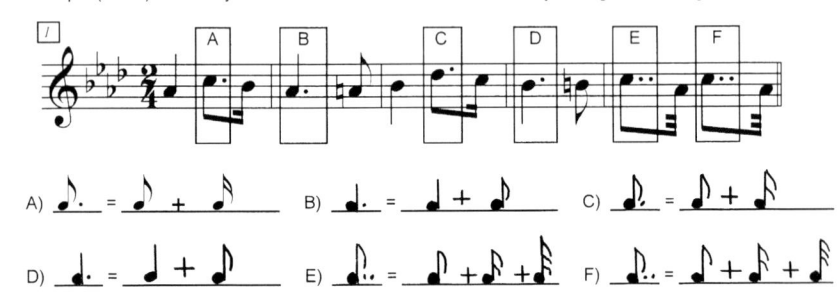

REST VALUE REVIEW - INCLUDING DOTTED RESTS and DOUBLE DOTTED RESTS

It is important to understand that **Rests Have Rules**. While technically each dotted note (or double dotted note) has a corresponding dotted rest (or double dotted rest) value, these types of rests can be used ONLY in specific rhythm situations.

To simplify this complex rhythmic concept, follow these **4 Rest Rules**:

Rule #1: Do not use dotted rests in Simple Time.
Rule #2: Do not use double dotted rests in Simple Time or in Compound Time.
Rule #3: In Compound Time, a dotted rest is used for a complete Compound Basic Beat.
   (Do not use a dotted rest for an incomplete Compound Basic Beat.)
Rule #4: In Compound Time, a dotted rest can also be used to join a Strong · + weak ·
   (S· + w·) or a Medium · + weak · (M· + w·) Compound Basic Beat.

So-La Says: Using "Music + Math" Skills, observe how Double Dotted Rests "technically" have the same value as Double Dotted Notes.

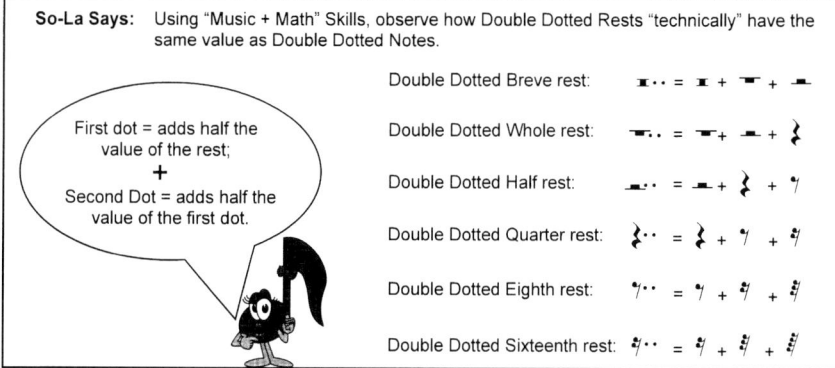

First dot = adds half the value of the rest;
+
Second Dot = adds half the value of the first dot.

Double Dotted Breve rest:
Double Dotted Whole rest:
Double Dotted Half rest:
Double Dotted Quarter rest:
Double Dotted Eighth rest:
Double Dotted Sixteenth rest:

♪ **Ti-Do Tip:** "Music + Math" means that Rests Have Rules. Do not use a dotted (or double dotted) rest simply because the values of the rests add together mathematically.

1. The rests in each measure in the upper (first) staff are INCORRECT. On the staff below, following the example in Measure 1, rewrite each rhythm using the correct rests.

Incorrect:

Correct:

2. Add the rest(s) below each bracket to complete each measure.

IRREGULAR GROUPING REVIEW

Irregular Groups are groups of notes (identified by a small number above or below the group) played in the time of a regular group of the same note value. The most common Irregular Group values are:

"Irregular Group"	In Simple Time	In Compound Time
Duplet (2)		2 = 3
Triplet (3)	3 = 2	
Quadruplet (4)		4 = 3
Quintuplet (5)	5 = 4	5 = 3 or 5 = 6
Sextuplet (6)	6 = 4	
Septuplet (7)	7 = 4	7 = 3 or 7 = 6

Review your **UMT Intermediate Rudiments Workbook**, Lesson 5.

While not common, Duplets and Quadruplets can be found in Simple Time, and Triplets can be found in Compound Time. The value of the irregular group will usually stay the same (Duplet: 2 = 3; Triplet: 3 = 2; Quadruplet: 4 = 3).

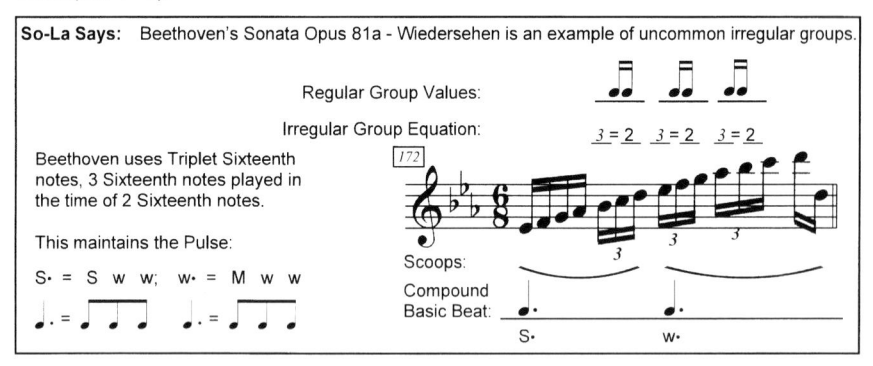

So-La Says: Beethoven's Sonata Opus 81a - Wiedersehen is an example of uncommon irregular groups.

Regular Group Values:

Irregular Group Equation: 3 = 2   3 = 2   3 = 2

Beethoven uses Triplet Sixteenth notes, 3 Sixteenth notes played in the time of 2 Sixteenth notes.

This maintains the Pulse:

S· = S w w; w· = M w w

Scoops:
Compound Basic Beat:
S·   w·

1. a) Scoop each Compound Basic Beat and write the Compound Basic Beat below each scoop.
   b) Analyze the Irregular Groups by writing the "Irregular Group Equation" and the regular group values.

Regular Group Values:

Irregular Group Equation: 4 = 3   2 = 3   7 = 3   5 = 3

Scoops:
Compound Basic Beat:
S·   w·   S·   w·

"MUSIC + MATH" and IRREGULAR GROUP EQUATION VALUES

To identify the Irregular Group Equation, discover what **single note value** is required to complete the rhythm where the Irregular Group is placed. Use Music + Math to find the value of the Irregular Group Equation.

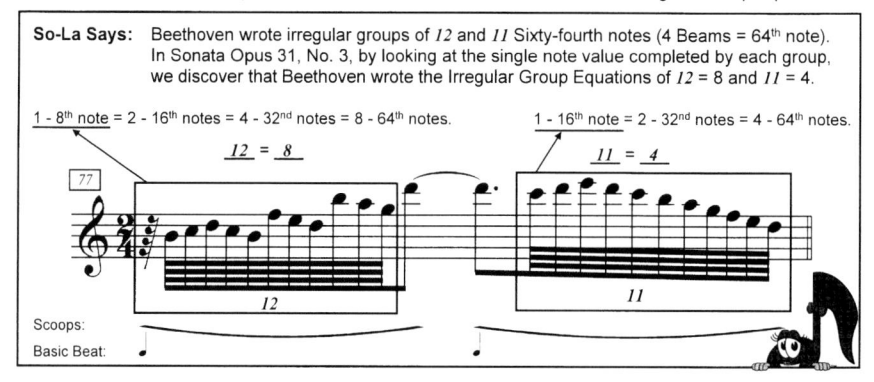

So-La Says: Beethoven wrote irregular groups of *12* and *11* Sixty-fourth notes (4 Beams = 64th note). In Sonata Opus 31, No. 3, by looking at the single note value completed by each group, we discover that Beethoven wrote the Irregular Group Equations of *12* = 8 and *11* = 4.

1 - 8th note = 2 - 16th notes = 4 - 32nd notes = 8 - 64th notes.   1 - 16th note = 2 - 32nd notes = 4 - 64th notes.

$$\underline{12} = \underline{8} \qquad \underline{11} = \underline{4}$$

1. a) Scoop each Basic Beat and write the Basic Beat below each scoop.
   b) Analyze the Irregular Groups by writing the "Irregular Group Equation" and the regular group values.

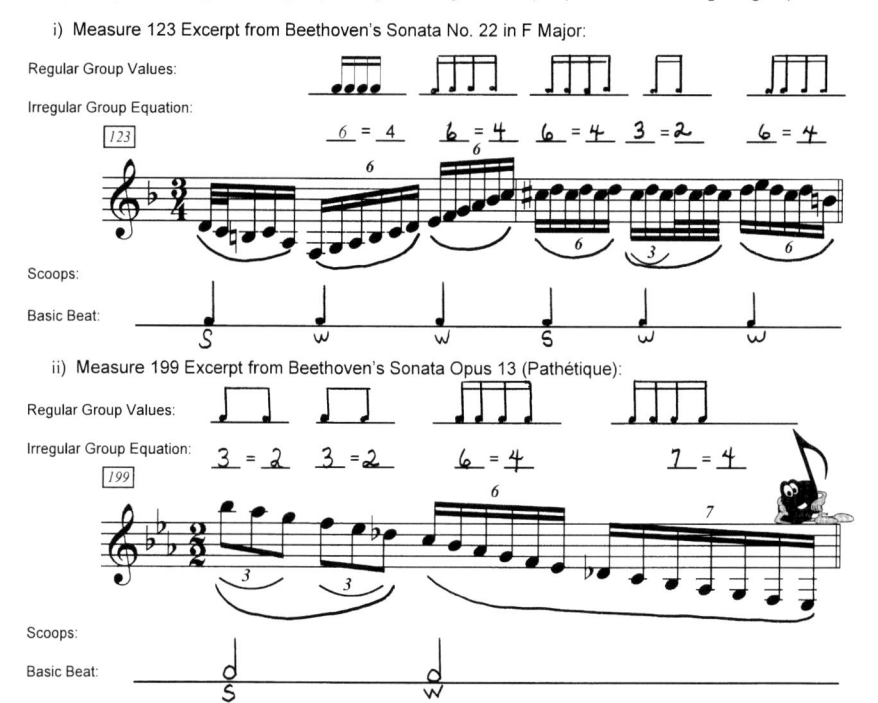

   i) Measure 123 Excerpt from Beethoven's Sonata No. 22 in F Major:

   Irregular Group Equation: $\underline{6} = \underline{4} \quad \underline{6} = \underline{4} \quad \underline{6} = \underline{4} \quad \underline{3} = \underline{2} \quad \underline{6} = \underline{4}$

   ii) Measure 199 Excerpt from Beethoven's Sonata Opus 13 (Pathétique):

   Irregular Group Equation: $\underline{3} = \underline{2} \quad \underline{3} = \underline{2} \quad \underline{6} = \underline{4} \quad \underline{7} = \underline{4}$

SCALES, SCALE DEGREES and KEY RELATIONSHIP REVIEW

Review Pages 16 and 17 of the **Ultimate Music Theory LEVEL 6 Supplemental Workbook**: Key Relationship Review and Scale Review.

Relative Major and minor keys: Same Key Signature, different Tonic Notes.

Parallel (or Tonic) Major and minor keys: Same Tonic Note, different Key Signatures.

Enharmonic Parallel (or Tonic) Major and/or minor keys: Same Pitch, different letter names.

Enharmonic Relative Major and/or minor keys: Begin on the same pitch as the relative Major or minor, but use different letter names.

So-La Says: When asked to write a **Relative** Major or minor scale, a **Parallel** (Tonic) Major or minor scale, an **Enharmonic Tonic** scale or an **Enharmonic Relative** scale:

Step #1: Identify the name of the scale based on the question. (To support the identification of Key Relationships, write the Circle of Fifths on your Whiteboard.)

Step #2: Write the scale. Follow the instructions to use accidentals or to use a Key Signature (and any necessary accidentals for a harmonic or melodic scale).

1. Identify the name of the scale based on the question. Write the scale as directed (using a Key Signature or accidentals), ascending and descending. Use whole notes.

a) The Parallel (Tonic) minor, melodic form, of A♭ Major in the Treble Clef using accidentals.
   Name of scale: a♭ minor melodic

b) The Enharmonic Parallel Major (Tonic Major) of c♯ minor in the Bass Clef using a Key Signature.
   Name of scale: D♭ Major

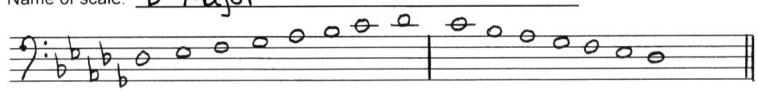

c) The Relative minor, harmonic form, of F♯ Major in the Treble Clef using accidentals.
   Name of scale: d♯ minor harmonic

d) The Enharmonic Relative minor scale, natural form, of C♯ Major in the Bass Clef using a Key Signature.
   Name of scale: b♭ minor natural

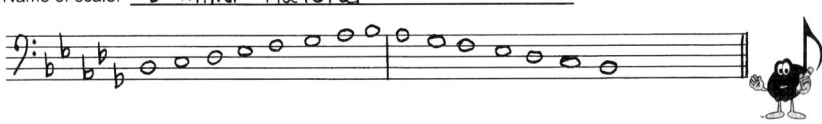

SCALES REVIEW - WRITING SCALES BASED ON "HINTS"

Be a Detective! Use the Scale Degree Names or the Circle of Fifths to identify which Scale to write.

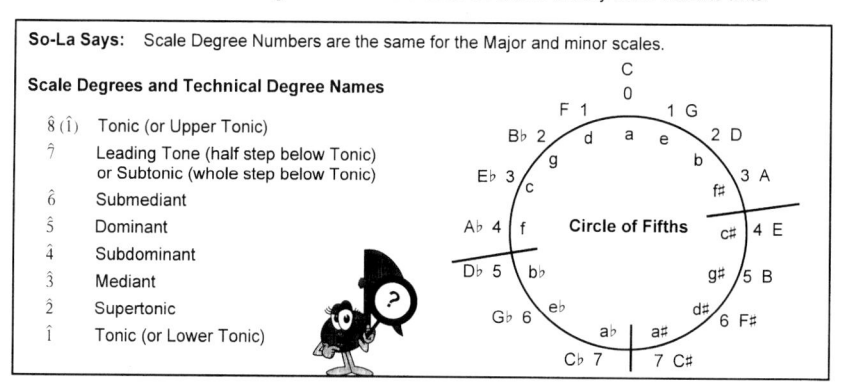

So-La Says: Scale Degree Numbers are the same for the Major and minor scales.

Scale Degrees and Technical Degree Names

- $\hat{8}\,(\hat{1})$ Tonic (or Upper Tonic)
- $\hat{7}$ Leading Tone (half step below Tonic) or Subtonic (whole step below Tonic)
- $\hat{6}$ Submediant
- $\hat{5}$ Dominant
- $\hat{4}$ Subdominant
- $\hat{3}$ Mediant
- $\hat{2}$ Supertonic
- $\hat{1}$ Tonic (or Lower Tonic)

Circle of Fifths:
C 0, F 1, G 1, Bb 2, D 2, Eb 3, A 3, Ab 4, E 4, Db 5, B 5, Gb 6, F# 6, Cb 7, C# 7

♪ **Ti-Do Tip:** Review Pages 18 and 19 of the **LEVEL 6 Supplemental Workbook**: Scale Degree Review - Leading Tone or Subtonic, and Writing Scales Based on a Technical Degree Name.

1. Identify the name of the scale based on the question. Write the scale as directed (using a Key Signature or accidentals), ascending and descending. Use whole notes.

a) The Major scale with B♭ as the Leading Tone in the Bass Clef using a Key Signature.
   Name of scale: __Cb Major__

b) The natural minor scale with B♭ as the Subtonic in the Treble Clef using accidentals.
   Name of scale: __C minor natural__

c) The melodic minor scale with a Key Signature of 5 flats in the Bass Clef using accidentals.
   Name of scale: __bb minor Melodic__

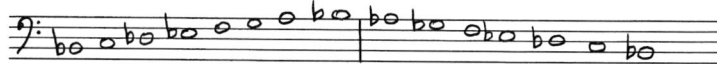

♪ **Ti-Do Time:** Your Teacher will play the scales on Pages 12 & 13. Identify the scale as a Major, natural minor, harmonic minor or melodic minor scale.

CHROMATIC SCALES REVIEW

A **Chromatic scale** is a 13 note scale written with 12 different pitches of a half step. Review different ways to write standard notations of a Chromatic Scale in the **UMT Intermediate Workbook** Pages 48 and 49.

The **3 Rules for Writing a Chromatic Scale** are:

Rule #1: The lowest note and the highest note must be the same note/letter name (written only once).

Rule #2: Each letter name can be written once or twice in a row, but never three times in a row in an ascending or a descending octave (or part of the Chromatic scale).

Rule #3: Each half step is either Chromatic (same letter name) or Diatonic (different letter name).

So-La Says: Keep it Simple! Follow these 3 Steps to write a Chromatic Scale correctly:

To write a "Harmonic" Chromatic scale starting on D:

Step #1: Identify the Tonic (I) note and the Dominant (V) note for the Major key of the given note.

Step #2: In the ascending scale, write a single Tonic, Dominant and Upper Tonic note, and two of all the other pitches. Add a bar line. Continue in the descending scale with a single Dominant and Lower Tonic, and two of all the other pitches.

V = A
I = D

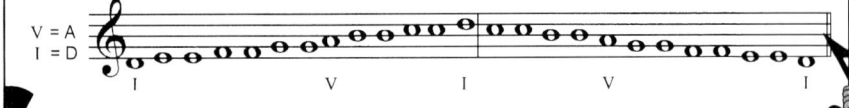

Step #3: Add the necessary accidentals to create either a Chromatic Half Step or a Diatonic Half Step between each note. (Do not alter any note/letter names.)

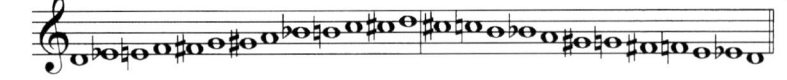

---

1. Write the following Chromatic scales ascending and descending. Use accidentals. Use whole notes.

   a) Chromatic scale starting on C in the Bass Clef.

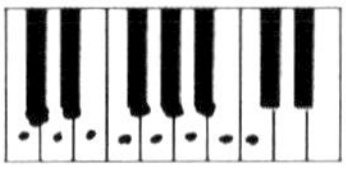

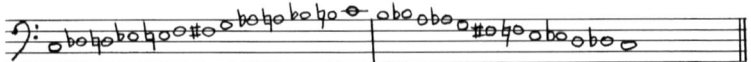

   b) Chromatic scale starting on D♭ in the Treble Clef.

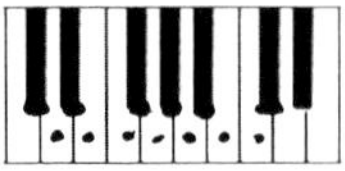

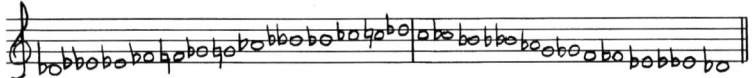

UltimateMusicTheory.com © Copyright 2017 Gloryland Publishing. All Rights Reserved.

WHOLE TONE SCALES REVIEW

A **Whole Tone scale** is a 7 note scale written with 6 different pitches of a whole step. Review Whole Tone scales in the **UMT Intermediate Workbook** Page 95.

The **3 Rules for Writing a Whole Tone Scale** are:

Rule #1: Use 6 different letter names. (One letter name in the octave will be omitted.) The lowest note and highest note must be the same note/letter name. Ascending and descending notes are the same.

Rule #2: 5 whole steps will be Diatonic Whole Steps (intervals of a Major 2) and 1 will be a diminished 3rd (the omitted letter name creates the pitch of a whole step, using the interval of a skip, a 3rd).

Rule #3: White key notes must be "naturals", and only black keys will use accidentals. Black key notes will be either all sharps or all flats (ascending and descending). Do not mix sharps and flat in a scale.

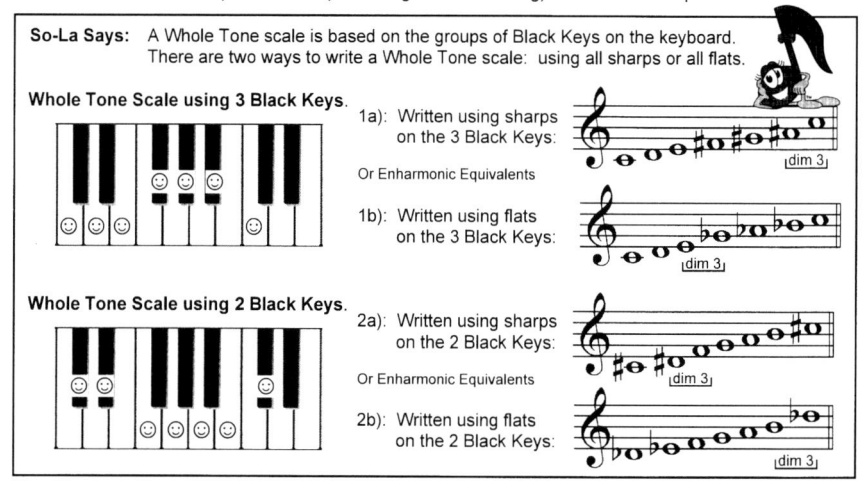

So-La Says: A Whole Tone scale is based on the groups of Black Keys on the keyboard. There are two ways to write a Whole Tone scale: using all sharps or all flats.

Whole Tone Scale using 3 Black Keys.

1a): Written using sharps on the 3 Black Keys:

Or Enharmonic Equivalents

1b): Written using flats on the 3 Black Keys:

Whole Tone Scale using 2 Black Keys.

2a): Written using sharps on the 2 Black Keys:

Or Enharmonic Equivalents

2b): Written using flats on the 2 Black Keys:

1. Write the following Whole Tone scales ascending and descending. Use accidentals. Use whole notes. Identify and label the interval of a dim 3 directly below the staff as: ⌊ dim 3 ⌋ .

   a) Whole Tone scale starting on E in the Bass Clef. Use flats.

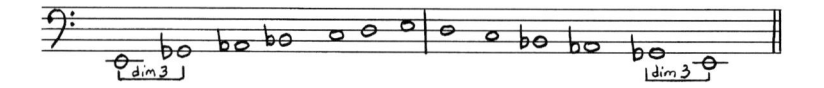

   b) Whole Tone scale starting on E in the Treble Clef. Use sharps.

OCTATONIC SCALES REVIEW

An **Octatonic scale** is a 9 note scale written with 8 different pitches that alternate between a Half Step (HS) and a Whole Step (WS). Review Octatonic scales in the **UMT Intermediate Workbook** Page 97.

The **3 Rules for Writing an Octatonic Scale** are:

Rule #1: All 7 letter names are used once, plus a repeated Tonic (first and last Tonic note of the scale must be the same note/letter name), and 1 letter name is repeated twice (in a row) for a total of 9 notes.

Rule #2: Alternate distances of whole steps and half steps. When written correctly, an Octatonic scale will have 4 Diatonic Whole Steps, 3 Diatonic Half Steps and 1 Chromatic Half Step.

Rule #3: The Tonic letter name may NOT be written twice in a row. Do not begin or end on a Chromatic HS or WS. Do not skip any letter names. Ascending and descending note names are the same.

So-La Says: There will be more than one correct "way" to write each Octatonic scale.

3 CORRECT ways to write an Octatonic scale starting on C:

*TIP: The Whole Step or Half Step Pattern at the top will repeat to continue the descending scale using the same note names.

Beginning with a Half Step:

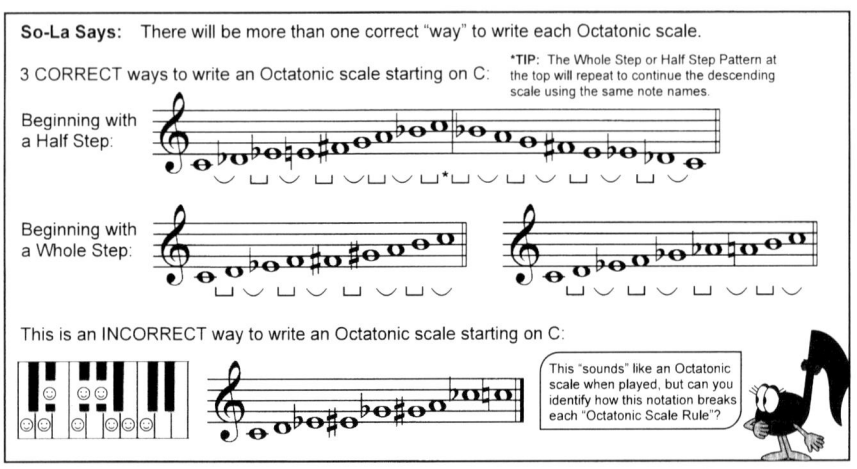

Beginning with a Whole Step:

This is an INCORRECT way to write an Octatonic scale starting on C:

This "sounds" like an Octatonic scale when played, but can you identify how this notation breaks each "Octatonic Scale Rule"?

♫ **Ti-Do Tip:** Unless the instructions specifically say to begin with a Whole Step or a Half Step, it is acceptable to begin with either a Whole Step or a Half Step.

1. Write the following Octatonic scales ascending and descending. Use accidentals. Use whole notes. There will be more than one correct answer.

   a) Octatonic scale starting on E in the Bass Clef. Begin with a Whole Step.

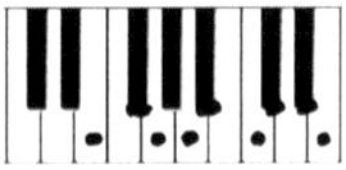

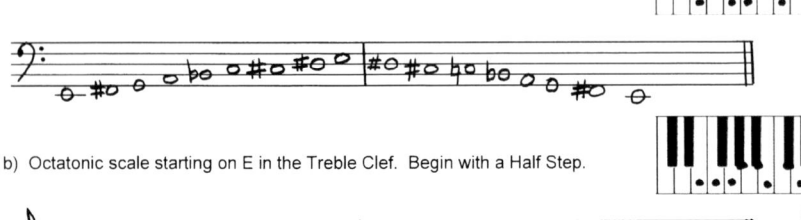

   b) Octatonic scale starting on E in the Treble Clef. Begin with a Half Step.

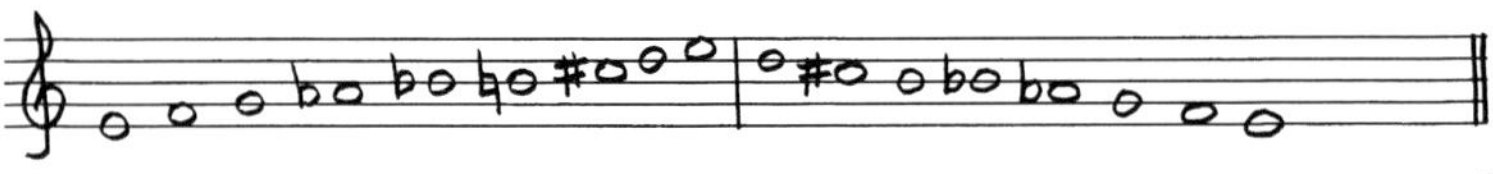

MAJOR and MINOR PENTATONIC SCALES REVIEW

A **Pentatonic scale** is a 6 note scale written with 5 different pitches (three intervals of a Major 2 and two intervals of a minor 3). Review the two common forms of Pentatonic scales, the Major Pentatonic scale and the minor Pentatonic scale, in the **UMT Intermediate Workbook** Page 96.

The **3 Rules for Writing a Pentatonic Scale** are:

Rule #1: Both Major and minor Pentatonic scales will use 5 different letter names. The interval patterns of Major 2 and minor 3 will be in a different order. The lowest note and the highest note (Tonic) must be the same note/letter name.

Rule #2: The pattern of a Major Pentatonic scale is: Major 2, Major 2, minor 3, Major 2, minor 3. The pattern of a minor Pentatonic scale is: minor 3, Major 2, Major 2, minor 3, Major 2.

Rule #3: The ascending and descending note names will be the same.

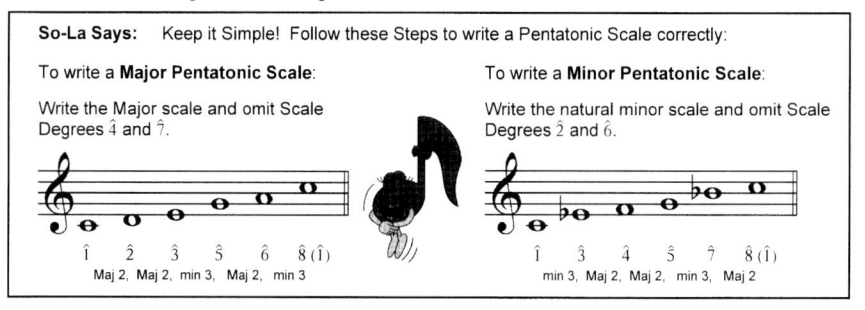

> **So-La Says:** Keep it Simple! Follow these Steps to write a Pentatonic Scale correctly:
>
> To write a **Major Pentatonic Scale**:
> Write the Major scale and omit Scale Degrees $\hat{4}$ and $\hat{7}$.
>
> To write a **Minor Pentatonic Scale**:
> Write the natural minor scale and omit Scale Degrees $\hat{2}$ and $\hat{6}$.

A **Major** Pentatonic scale starts with a **Major 2** and a **minor** Pentatonic scale starts with a **minor 3**.

1. Write the following Pentatonic scales ascending and descending. Use accidentals. Use whole notes. Write the scale degree number directly below each note.

   a) Major Pentatonic scale starting on E in the Bass Clef.

   b) Minor Pentatonic scale starting on E in the Treble Clef.

   c) Minor Pentatonic scale starting on C sharp in the Bass Clef.

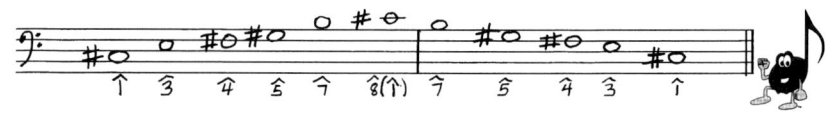

BLUES SCALES REVIEW

A **Blues scale** is a 7 note scale written with 6 different pitches. (There will be only 5 letter names used.) Review Blues scales in the **UMT Intermediate Workbook** Page 97.

The **3 Rules for Writing a Blues Scale** are:

Rule #1: The Blues scale uses 5 letter names based on the minor pentatonic scale, adding the raised $\hat{4}$ or lowered $\hat{5}$ scale degree. This is often referred to as the "Blue note". The first note and last note of the scale must be written with the same note/letter name.

Rule #2: Whether you "Raise the 4" or "Lower the 5", the scale will sound the same. Either is correct.
  Raise the ↑$\hat{4}$ - Scale Degree $\hat{4}$ is written twice. **Lower the** ↓$\hat{5}$ - Scale Degree $\hat{5}$ is written twice.

Rule #3: The ascending and descending note names will be the same.

So-La Says: Keep it Simple! Follow these 2 Steps to write a Blues Scale correctly:

Step #1: Write the minor pentatonic scale (or write the natural minor scale, omitting Scale Degrees $\hat{2}$ and $\hat{6}$). Leave a space between Scale Degrees $\hat{4}$ and $\hat{5}$.

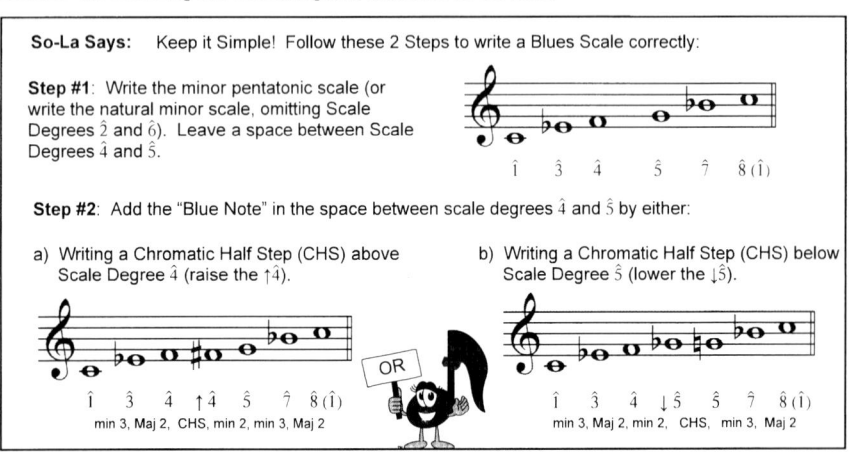

Step #2: Add the "Blue Note" in the space between scale degrees $\hat{4}$ and $\hat{5}$ by either:

a) Writing a Chromatic Half Step (CHS) above Scale Degree $\hat{4}$ (raise the ↑$\hat{4}$).

b) Writing a Chromatic Half Step (CHS) below Scale Degree $\hat{5}$ (lower the ↓$\hat{5}$).

min 3, Maj 2, CHS, min 2, min 3, Maj 2   OR   min 3, Maj 2, min 2, CHS, min 3, Maj 2

♪ **Ti-Do Tip:** Unless the instructions specifically say to raise the ↑$\hat{4}$ or to lower the ↓$\hat{5}$, it is acceptable to write a Blues scale either way (providing more than one correct answer).

1. Write the following Blues scales ascending and descending. Use accidentals. Use whole notes. Write the scale degree number directly below each note.

   a) Blues scale starting on E in the Treble Clef. Raise the ↑$\hat{4}$.

   $\hat{1}$ $\hat{3}$ $\hat{4}$ ↑$\hat{4}$ $\hat{5}$ $\hat{7}$ $\hat{8}(\hat{1})$ $\hat{7}$ $\hat{5}$ ↑$\hat{4}$ $\hat{4}$ $\hat{3}$ $\hat{1}$

   b) Blues scale starting on E in the Bass Clef. Lower the ↓$\hat{5}$.

   $\hat{1}$ $\hat{3}$ $\hat{4}$ ↓$\hat{5}$ $\hat{5}$ $\hat{7}$ $\hat{8}(\hat{1})$ $\hat{7}$ $\hat{5}$ ↓$\hat{5}$ $\hat{4}$ $\hat{3}$ $\hat{1}$

SCALE IDENTIFICATION REVIEW

Use the following chart to quickly identify the type of scale:

Number of Notes:	Ti-Do Tip:	Type of Scale:
6 notes (5 plus repeated Tonic)	First interval is a Major 2	Major Pentatonic
6 notes (5 plus repeated Tonic)	First interval is a minor 3	Minor Pentatonic
7 notes (6 plus repeated Tonic)	Seven different notes in a row	Whole Tone Scale
7 notes (6 plus repeated Tonic)	Scale Degree $\hat{4}$ written twice or Scale Degree $\hat{5}$ written twice	Blues Scale
9 notes (8 plus repeated Tonic)	Alternating between HS and WS includes one chromatic half step	Octatonic Scale
13 notes (12 plus repeated Tonic)	All distances are half steps (chromatic or diatonic)	Chromatic Scale

So-La Says: A scale with 8 notes (7 plus repeated Tonic) will be either Major, natural minor, harmonic minor or melodic minor.

1. Name the following scales as Major Pentatonic, minor Pentatonic, Whole Tone, Blues, Octatonic or Chromatic.

a) Octatonic

b) Chromatic

c) Major Pentatonic

d) Blues Scale

e) Whole Tone

f) minor Pentatonic

INTERVAL REVIEW - WRITING ABOVE A NOTE

An Interval is the distance in pitch between two notes. Review Intervals in the **UMT Intermediate Workbook** Lesson 6 (Pages 73 - 78).

The Interval **Number** is the size of the interval, identified by counting each line and space from the lower note to the higher note. (The lower note is always counted as 1.)

The **Type** or **Quality** of the interval is whether the interval is Major, minor, Perfect, Augmented or diminished. The Type/Quality of an interval is determined by the Major Key Signature of the lower note.

The Type/Quality of an interval **changes** when moving a chromatic half step (semitone):

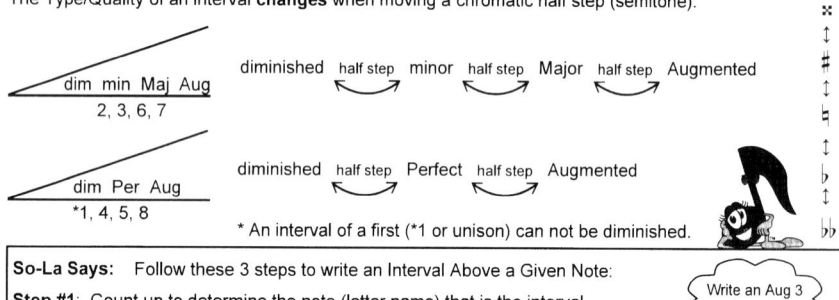

dim min Maj Aug
2, 3, 6, 7

diminished — half step → minor — half step → Major — half step → Augmented

dim Per Aug
*1, 4, 5, 8

diminished — half step → Perfect — half step → Augmented

* An interval of a first (*1 or unison) can not be diminished.

So-La Says: Follow these 3 steps to write an Interval Above a Given Note:

Step #1: Count up to determine the note (letter name) that is the interval number above the given note. Write that note without an accidental.

Step #2: Determine the type/quality of the interval (Maj, min, Per, Aug or dim) based upon the Major Key Signature of the lower note.

Step #3: Using accidentals (𝄪, ♯, ♮, ♭, 𝄫), move one chromatic half step at a time to adjust the top note until the correct interval is formed.

Do not change the given note.

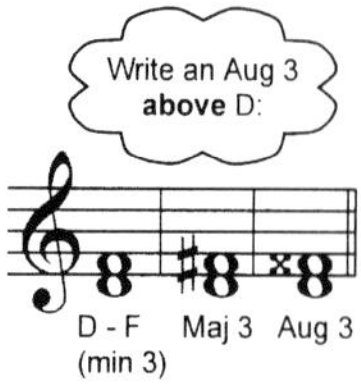

Write an Aug 3 above D:

D - F   Maj 3   Aug 3
(min 3)

♩ **Ti-Do Tip:** Intervals can be written with or without a **Key Signature**. The accidentals in the Key Signature may affect the interval note names and their type/quality.
Harmonic Intervals are written vertically, one above the other.
Melodic Intervals are written separately, one beside the other.

1. Write each harmonic interval above the given note. Use whole notes.

   dim 5   min 7   Aug 2   Maj 6   Aug 4   dim 8

2. Observing the Key Signature, write each melodic interval above the given note. Use whole notes.

   Maj 3   Per 1   min 6   Per 4   dim 5   Aug 7

INTERVAL REVIEW - WRITING BELOW A NOTE

The **3 Rules for Placement of Accidentals in a Harmonic Interval** are:

Rule #1: For Harmonic Intervals of a 1, 2, 3, 4, 5 and 6: when both notes have accidentals, the accidental is written closer to the higher (top) note and further away from the lower (bottom) note.

Rule #2: For Harmonic Intervals of a 7 and 8: when both notes have accidentals, the accidentals are written lined up vertically (above each other).

Rule #3: When writing a Harmonic Interval, and there is **no room for the correct placement of accidentals**, it is acceptable to place the accidental further away from the upper note.

For a **Harmonic Augmented 1**, in order to maintain the integrity of the Harmonic Interval (noteheads are together, "touching"), two accidentals will be required. The first accidental will apply to the first note; the second accidental will apply to the second note.

In a Harmonic Augmented 1, the lower pitched note is written first and then the higher pitched note. A natural sign will be placed at the beginning if the lower pitched note is the "natural" note (white key).

So-La Says: Follow these 3 steps to write an Interval Below a Given Note:

Step #1: Count down to determine the note (letter name) that is the interval number below the given note. Write that note without an accidental.

Step #2: Determine the type/quality of the interval (Maj, min, Per, Aug or dim) based upon the Major Key Signature of the lower note.

Step #3: Using accidentals (𝄪, ♯, ♮, ♭, ♭♭), move one chromatic half step at a time to adjust the lower note until the correct interval is formed.

Do not change the given note.

♪ **Ti-Do Tip:** Intervals within an octave are called **Simple Intervals**. The smallest Simple Interval is a Perfect 1 (or Perfect Unison). The largest Simple Interval is a Perfect 8 (or Perfect Octave).

1. Write each harmonic interval below the given note. Use whole notes.

   dim 6   Maj 7   Per 5   Aug 1   Maj 3   min 2

2. Observing the Key Signature, write each melodic interval below the given note. Use whole notes.

   dim 8   Maj 2   Per 4   Aug 7   min 6   Aug 1

♪ **Ti-Do Time:** Your Teacher will play the intervals on Pages 20 and 21. Identify the interval (number and type/quality). Is the interval harmonic or melodic?

INTERVAL INVERSIONS REVIEW

An **Inversion of a Simple Interval** occurs when the interval is turned upside down. When an interval is inverted, its Quality & Quantity will change. "**Quantity**" refers to the number of letter names that an interval encompasses (covers). Review Interval Inversions in the **UMT Intermediate Workbook** on Page 78.

The **3 Rules for Inverting an Interval** are:

Rule #1: Transpose the lower note up one octave (bottom/lower note moves to become the top/higher note) or transpose the higher note down one octave (top note moves to become the bottom note).

Rule #2: When inverting an interval, the **Quality** (type/quality) of the interval changes:

> Major becomes minor; minor becomes Major;
>
> Augmented becomes diminished; diminished becomes Augmented;
>
> Perfect stays Perfect.

Rule #3: The combined **Quantity** (the combined value of the Simple Interval number and the inversion number) will always equal 9. (Per 4 when inverted becomes a Per 5. Quantity 4 + 5 = 9)

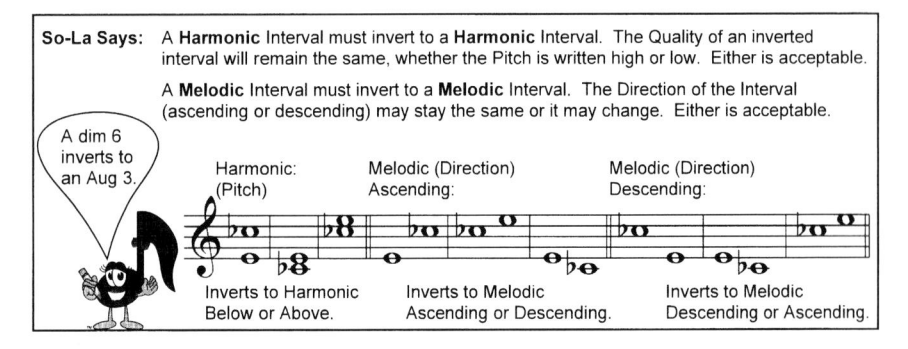

So-La Says: A **Harmonic** Interval must invert to a **Harmonic** Interval. The Quality of an inverted interval will remain the same, whether the Pitch is written high or low. Either is acceptable.

A **Melodic** Interval must invert to a **Melodic** Interval. The Direction of the Interval (ascending or descending) may stay the same or it may change. Either is acceptable.

A dim 6 inverts to an Aug 3.

Harmonic: (Pitch) — Inverts to Harmonic Below or Above.

Melodic (Direction) Ascending: — Inverts to Melodic Ascending or Descending.

Melodic (Direction) Descending: — Inverts to Melodic Descending or Ascending.

1. a) Name each harmonic interval.
   b) Invert each interval. (There will be more than one correct notation.) Name the inversion.

   min 7   Maj 2   dim 3   Aug 6   Per 4   Per 5   Aug 1   dim 8

2. a) Name each melodic interval.
   b) Invert each interval. (There will be more than one correct notation.) Name the inversion.

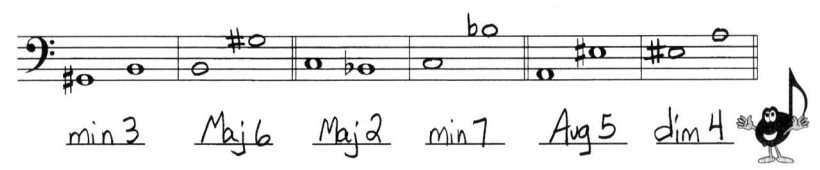

   min 3   Maj 6   Maj 2   min 7   Aug 5   dim 4

ENHARMONIC EQUIVALENT INTERVALS REVIEW

Enharmonic Equivalent Intervals are intervals that, when played, sound at the same pitch but are written using either a different upper (top) note or a different lower (bottom) note (an Enharmonic Equivalent). Review Enharmonic Equivalent Intervals in the **UMT LEVEL 6 Supplemental Workbook** on Page 26.

The **3 Rules for Writing Enharmonic Equivalent Intervals** are:

Rule #1: **Read the instructions.** To rewrite an Enharmonic Equivalent Interval, observe whether the upper note is to be changed enharmonically or whether the lower note is to be changed enharmonically.

Rule #2: A note changed to its Enharmonic Equivalent will use a neighboring (next door) letter name, either the letter name above or the letter name below. Do not skip a letter name.

Rule #3: When selecting the Enharmonic Equivalent Note, it is important that the note selected must create a Standard Interval Quality of an Aug, Per, Maj, min or dim.

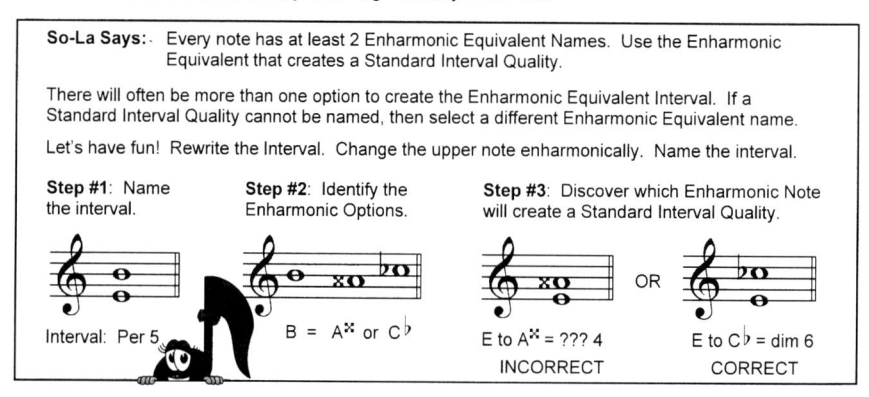

> **So-La Says:** Every note has at least 2 Enharmonic Equivalent Names. Use the Enharmonic Equivalent that creates a Standard Interval Quality.
>
> There will often be more than one option to create the Enharmonic Equivalent Interval. If a Standard Interval Quality cannot be named, then select a different Enharmonic Equivalent name.
>
> Let's have fun! Rewrite the Interval. Change the upper note enharmonically. Name the interval.
>
> **Step #1**: Name the interval.
> Interval: Per 5
>
> **Step #2**: Identify the Enharmonic Options.
> B = A$^{\times}$ or C♭
>
> **Step #3**: Discover which Enharmonic Note will create a Standard Interval Quality.
> E to A$^{\times}$ = ??? 4   OR   E to C♭ = dim 6
> INCORRECT   CORRECT

♪ **Ti-Do Tip:** Use your UMT Whiteboard to simplify identification of Enharmonic Equivalent options.

1. a) Name each interval.
   b) Rewrite each interval, changing the lower note enharmonically. Name the new interval.

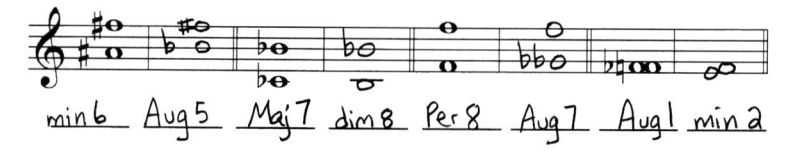

   min 6   Aug 5   Maj 7   dim 8   Per 8   Aug 7   Aug 1   min 2

2. a) Name each interval.
   b) Rewrite each interval, changing the upper note enharmonically. Name the new interval.

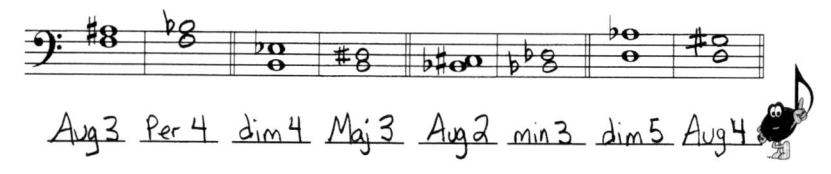

   Aug 3   Per 4   dim 4   Maj 3   Aug 2   min 3   dim 5   Aug 4

TRANSPOSITION - INTERVAL of TRANSPOSITION and NEW KEY

Transposition occurs when music is written or played at a different pitch. Review Transposition - Major Key to Major Key in the **UMT Intermediate Workbook** in Lesson 11.

The **3 Rules for Transposition** are:

Rule #1: Name the original key. Observing the Interval of Transposition, name the new key. The interval of transposition can be any interval either above or below the Tonic of the original key. When transposing UP into a new key, all notes will be rewritten higher by the Interval of Transposition; when transposing DOWN into a new key, all notes will be rewritten lower.

Rule #2: The Type/Quality of the Interval of Transposition can be Maj, min, Per, Aug or dim. A melody will always transpose from Major key to Major key or minor key to minor key because every note is transposed by the exact same interval. *"Major key stays Major and minor key stays minor."*

Rule #3: The transposed melody will have the same Time Signature, dynamics and articulation as the original melody (but will follow the Stem Rules for the transposed notes).

If there is an accidental in the original melody, the transposed melody must have an accidental on that same note. This accidental may not be the same type of accidental (sharp, flat, natural, etc.) as in the given melody but it must perform the same function (either raising or lowering the note).

So-La Says: In order to transpose, the following information is required:
#1: The original key (given key).
#2: The Interval of Transposition and the direction of transposition, either up or down. (This is the interval between the Tonic of the given key and the Tonic of the new key.)
#3: The new key.

At this Level, to complete a Transposition question, the following will be provided:
a) the Interval of Transposition (to determine the new key) or
b) the new Key (to determine the Interval of Transposition).

♪ **Ti-Do Tip:** When provided with the names of both keys, determine the Interval of Transposition by determining the interval between the two Tonic notes. Observe the direction (up or down).

When provided with the Interval of Transposition, determine the Tonic of the new key by naming the notes of the Interval. Observe the direction (up or down).

1. Provide the Interval of Transposition for each of the following pairs of Keys.

Original Key Name	Interval of Transposition	New Key Name
c♯ minor	dim 3 (C♯ - E♭)	Up to e♭ minor
B Major	Aug 6 (D♭ - B)	Down to D♭ Major
D Major	Maj 7 (D - C♯)	Up to C♯ Major

2. Provide the New Key Name for each of the following transpositions.

Original Key Name	Interval of Transposition	New Key Name
e♭ minor	Up a Major 6 (E♭-C)	C minor
F♯ Major	Down an Augmented 4 (C-F♯)	C Major
g♯ minor	Down a Perfect 5 (C♯-G♯)	c♯ minor

TRANSPOSITION STEPS

When Transposing a Melody, all notes will move up or down by the same interval (Type/Quality and Interval Number). Using the correct Key Signature will ensure that all notes have moved by the same Type/Quality.

So-La Says: Follow the **3 Transposition Steps** to easily transpose a melody up or down.

Step #1: Identify the Key of the Given Melody, the Interval (and direction) of Transposition and the New Key. Write the Clef, the new Key Signature and the Time Signature for the New Key Melody.

Given Key: e minor
Interval: down Major 3
New Key: c minor

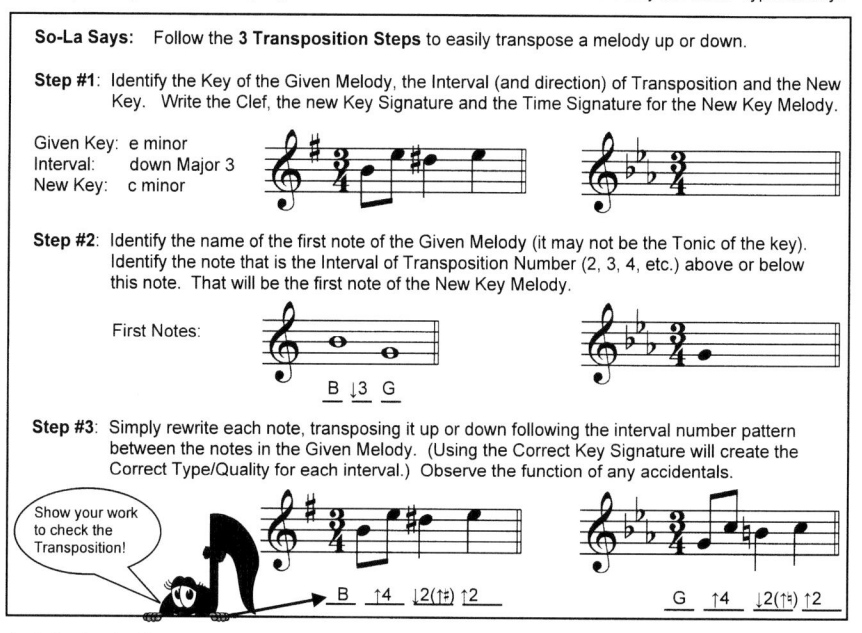

Step #2: Identify the name of the first note of the Given Melody (it may not be the Tonic of the key). Identify the note that is the Interval of Transposition Number (2, 3, 4, etc.) above or below this note. That will be the first note of the New Key Melody.

First Notes: B ↓3 G

Step #3: Simply rewrite each note, transposing it up or down following the interval number pattern between the notes in the Given Melody. (Using the Correct Key Signature will create the Correct Type/Quality for each interval.) Observe the function of any accidentals.

Show your work to check the Transposition!

B ↑4 ↓2(↑♮) ↑2   G ↑4 ↓2(↑♮) ↑2

1. Following the Transposition Steps, transpose the given melody down a Perfect 4. Show your work.

Given Key: d minor
Interval: Down Perfect 4
New Key: a minor

First Notes: A ↓4 E

A ↑3(↑♯) ↑3 ↓2   E ↑3(↑♮) ↑3 ↓2

2. Following the Transposition Steps, transpose the given melody up into D Major. Show your work.

Given Key: A♭ Major
Interval: Up Aug 4
New Key: D Major

First Notes: E♭ ↑4 A

E♭ ↑2 ↑2 ↑2   A ↑2 ↑2 ↑2

TRANSPOSITION - ACCIDENTALS

There are typically 3 reasons for the presence of an **accidental** in a melody (or a melodic excerpt):

#1: The melody is in a minor key and the accidental represents the raised $\hat{7}$ (the Leading Note) or the raised $\hat{6}$ and $\hat{7}$ (ascending melodic minor passage, the raised Submediant and Leading Note).

#2: The melodic excerpt has modulated into a new key (Major or minor) within the piece of music. Accidentals, instead of a new Key Signature, have been used to show the modulation. (Review the UMT LEVEL 6 Supplemental Workbook, Pages 42 and 43.)

#3: The Composer has used an accidental (or accidentals) simply for melodic direction or musical interest.

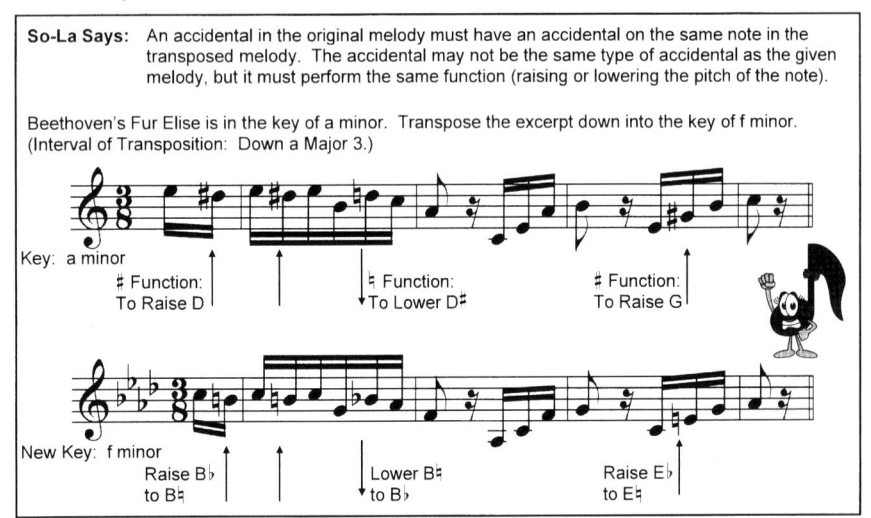

> **So-La Says:** An accidental in the original melody must have an accidental on the same note in the transposed melody. The accidental may not be the same type of accidental as the given melody, but it must perform the same function (raising or lowering the pitch of the note).
>
> Beethoven's Fur Elise is in the key of a minor. Transpose the excerpt down into the key of f minor. (Interval of Transposition: Down a Major 3.)

Key: a minor

♯ Function: To Raise D
♮ Function: To Lower D♯
♯ Function: To Raise G

New Key: f minor

Raise B♭ to B♮
Lower B♮ to B♭
Raise E♭ to E♮

A melody will sound at a higher pitch when transposed up, and at a lower pitch when transposed down.

1. Transpose mm. 9 - 10 of Friedrich Kuhlau's Sonata in C Major, Opus 88, No. 1, Mvt I down a Major 2 in the Bass Staff. (Interval of Transposition: Down a Major 2.) Name the New Key.

Key: C Major

New Key: __B♭ Major__

UltimateMusicTheory.com © Copyright 2017 Gloryland Publishing. All Rights Reserved.

TRANSPOSITION - DYNAMICS and ARTICULATION

When transposing a melody, all aspects of the given melody (dynamics, articulation, etc.) must be rewritten in the transposed melody. Observe the Stem Rule and proper placement of dynamics and articulation.

> **So-La Says:** Remember these **3 Tips for Transposition**:
>
> Tip #1: Write the Clef, new Key Signature, Time Signature and all bar lines first.
>
> Tip #2: Write the notes (check for any accidentals and direction of pitch), observing the Stem Rules for the transposed notes.
>
> Tip #3: Add any dynamics and articulation, observing the correct placement.

Transpose mm. 22 - 24 of Giovanni Platti's Sonata in C Major, Opus 1, No. 2, II Mvt down into G♭ Major. (Interval of Transposition: Down an Aug 4.)

Key: C Major

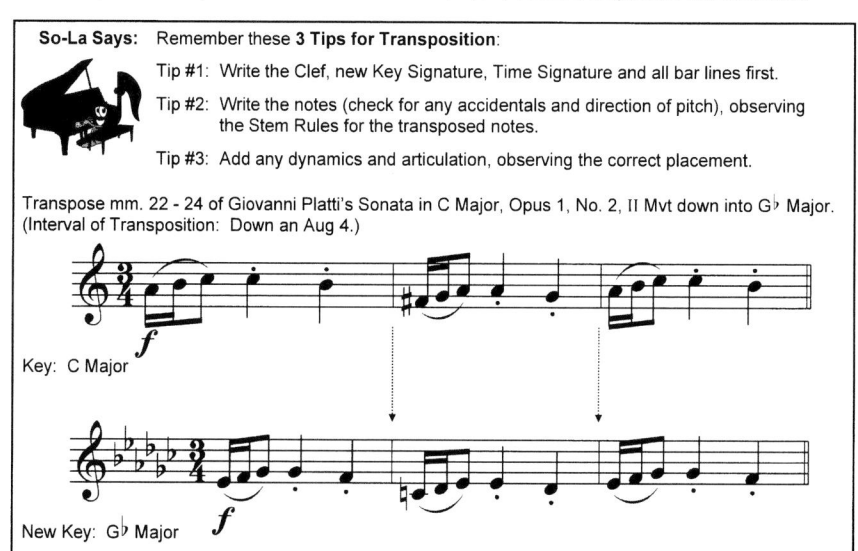

New Key: G♭ Major

On a single staff, dynamics are written below the Treble Clef and above the Bass Clef. On the Grand Staff, dynamics are written in the middle, between the Treble and Bass Staves.

1. Transpose mm. 22 - 24 of Giovanni Platti's Sonata in C Major, Opus 1, No. 2, Mvt II down a minor 3 in the Bass Staff. (Interval of Transposition: Down a minor 3.) Name the New Key.

Key: C Major

New Key: A Major

> ♪ **Ti-Do Time:** Your Teacher will play each Given Melody and the Transposed Melody (on Pages 25 - 27). Identify if the melody has been transposed up (at a higher pitch) or down (at a lower pitch).

TRIAD TYPE/QUALITY and ROOT/QUALITY CHORD SYMBOL REVIEW

A Triad is a three note chord. The lowest note of a root position triad (all lines or all spaces) is called the Root. A Root Position Triad consists of a third and a fifth above the Root. The Type/Quality of the triad (Major, minor, Augmented or diminished) is determined by the Type/Quality of the intervals above the root.

Triad Type/Quality:	Major Triad	Minor Triad	Augmented Triad	Diminished Triad
Type/Quality of 5th:	Perfect 5	Perfect 5	Augmented 5	diminished 5
Type/Quality of 3rd:	Major 3	minor 3	Major 3	minor 3
Root:	Root	Root	Root	Root

So-La Says: Root/Quality Chord Symbols use upper case letters to indicate the Root of the Triad, followed by a lower case letter or symbol to indicate the Quality of the Triad.

Triads: Root	Quality	Root/Quality Chord Symbols	
C	Major	C	(Root note of the Triad)
C	minor	Cm	(Root with an "m" for minor)
C	Augmented	C+ or Caug	(Root with a "+" or "aug")
C	diminished	C° or Cdim	(Root with a " ° " or "dim")

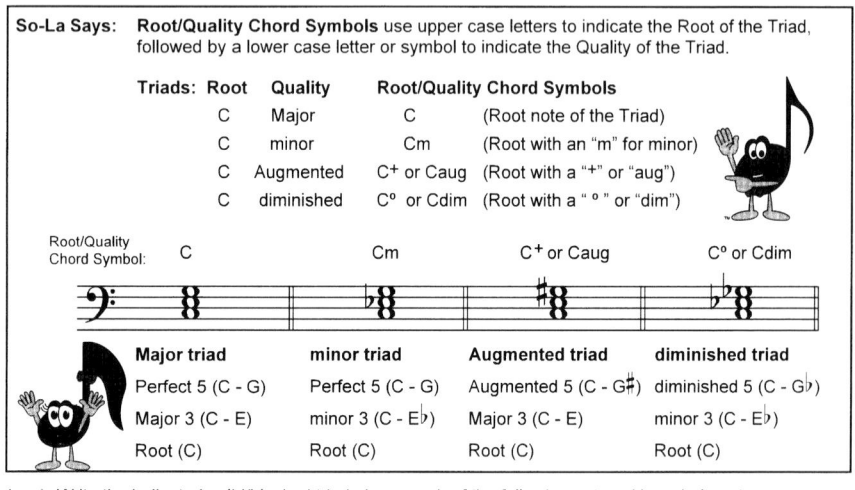

Root/Quality Chord Symbol: C   Cm   C+ or Caug   C° or Cdim

Major triad — Perfect 5 (C - G), Major 3 (C - E), Root (C)

minor triad — Perfect 5 (C - G), minor 3 (C - E♭), Root (C)

Augmented triad — Augmented 5 (C - G♯), Major 3 (C - E), Root (C)

diminished triad — diminished 5 (C - G♭), minor 3 (C - E♭), Root (C)

1. a) Write the indicated solid/blocked triad above each of the following notes. Use whole notes.
   b) Write the Root/Quality Chord Symbol above each triad.

Root/Quality Chord Symbol: G+ (Gaug), C+° (C#dim), B♭, Dm, B° (Bdim), A♭+ (A♭aug)

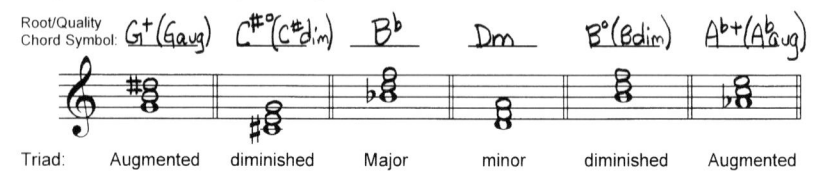

Triad: Augmented   diminished   Major   minor   diminished   Augmented

2. Write the solid/blocked triad for each Root/Quality Chord Symbol. Use whole notes.

Root/Quality Chord Symbol: Em   A+   D°   B   C♭+   F°

TRIAD POSITIONS and ROOT/QUALITY CHORD SYMBOLS

Review Pages 33 to 41 of the **Ultimate Music Theory LEVEL 5 Supplemental Workbook**: Triad Positions and Chord Symbols.

A **Slash Chord** is a Root/Quality Chord Symbol that indicates that a note other than the Root note is the lowest note of the triad (chord).

The letter name after the slash (" / ") is the name of the lowest note of the triad.

So-La Says: Observe the Proper Placement of Accidentals when writing Solid/Blocked Triads.

Proper placement of **2 accidentals**:
1st accidental - written closer to the top note;
2nd accidental - written further away from the bottom note.

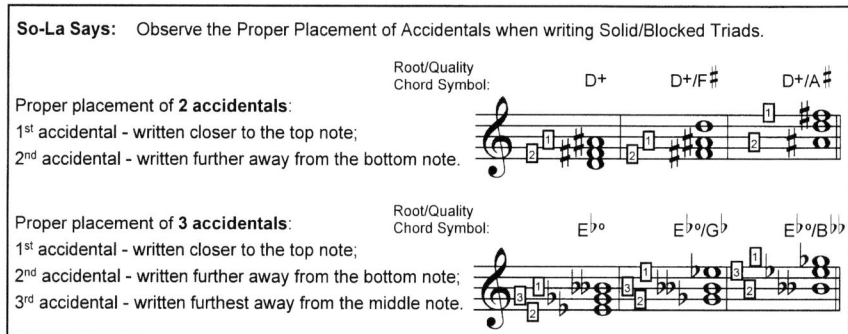

Root/Quality Chord Symbol: D+   D+/F♯   D+/A♯

Proper placement of **3 accidentals**:
1st accidental - written closer to the top note;
2nd accidental - written further away from the bottom note;
3rd accidental - written furthest away from the middle note.

Root/Quality Chord Symbol: E♭°   E♭°/G♭   E♭°/B♭♭

♪ **Ti-Do Tip:** When there is no room to write square [I'm thinking] brackets to show your work, use your Ultimate Music Theory Whiteboard to write your [I'm thinking] work.

1. a) Identify the Root, Type/Quality (Maj, min, Aug or dim) and Position (root pos, 1st inv or 2nd inv) of each of the following triads.
   b) Write the Root/Quality Chord Symbol above each triad.

Root/Quality Chord Symbol: E°/G   B   F+/C♯   Cm/E♭   B♭°/F♭

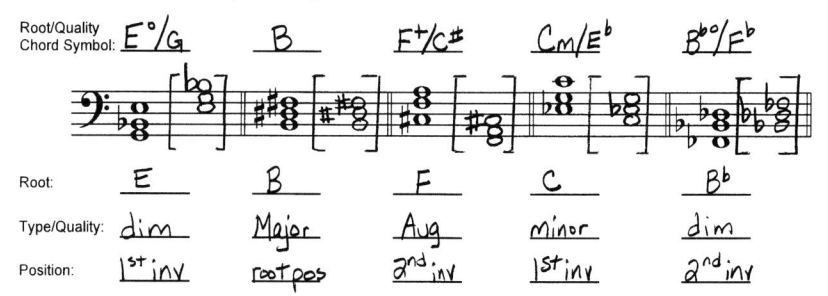

Root:	E	B	F	C	B♭
Type/Quality:	dim	Major	Aug	minor	dim
Position:	1st inv	root pos	2nd inv	1st inv	2nd inv

2. Write the solid/blocked triad for each Root/Quality Chord Symbol. Use whole notes.

Root/Quality Chord Symbol: F+/A   G♭   D+/A♯   A°/E♭   C♯m/E

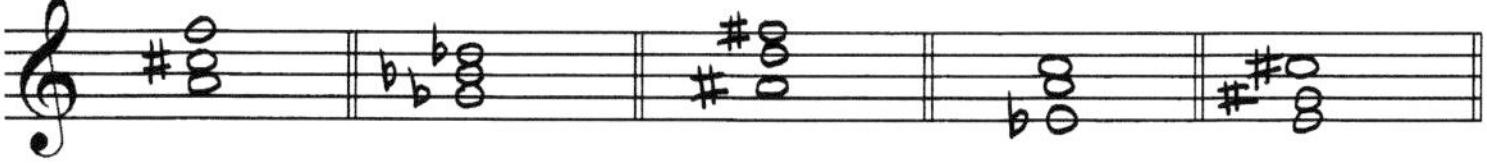

SCALE TRIADS - ROOT QUALITY CHORD SYMBOLS & FUNCTIONAL CHORD SYMBOLS

Root/Quality Chord Symbols use upper case letters to indicate the Root, followed by a lower case letter or symbol to indicate the Quality of the Triad. Triads can be built on any degree of a Major and minor scale.

Functional Chord Symbols use Roman Numerals (upper case and lower case) to show the Scale Degree on which the triad is built and the Type/Quality (Major, minor, Augmented or diminished) of the Triad.

Triads:	Root	Quality	Root/Quality	Functional Chord Symbols
	A	Major	A	Maj Triad = upper case Roman Numeral. (IV)
	A	minor	Am	min Triad = lower case Roman Numeral. (iv)
	G	Augmented	G+ or Gaug	Aug Triad = upper case Roman Numeral with a "+". (III+)
	D	diminished	D° or Ddim	dim Triad = lower case Roman Number with a " ° ". (vii°)

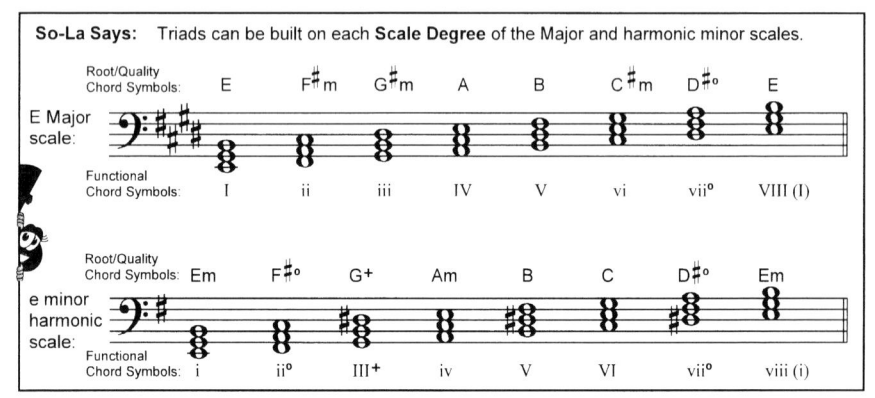

So-La Says: Triads can be built on each **Scale Degree** of the Major and harmonic minor scales.

E Major scale — Root/Quality Chord Symbols: E, F#m, G#m, A, B, C#m, D#°, E
Functional Chord Symbols: I, ii, iii, IV, V, vi, vii°, VIII (I)

e minor harmonic scale — Root/Quality Chord Symbols: Em, F#°, G+, Am, B, C, D#°, Em
Functional Chord Symbols: i, ii°, III+, iv, V, VI, vii°, viii (i)

♪ **Ti-Do Tip:** An accidental affects the note on that line or in that space until it is canceled by a bar line or by another accidental. When writing the triads of the harmonic minor scale, it is necessary to write the accidental for the raised Leading Tone on each of the 3 triads (III+, V and vii°).

1. Write the Root/Quality Chord Symbol above each triad and the Functional Chord Symbol below.

a) D♭ Major scale:
Root/Quality Chord Symbols: D♭, E♭m, Fm, G♭, A♭, B♭m, C°, D♭
Functional Chord Symbols: I, ii, iii, IV, V, vi, vii°, VIII (I)

b) b♭ minor harmonic scale:
Root/Quality Chord Symbols: B♭m, C°, D♭+, E♭m, F, G♭, A(♮)°, B♭m
Functional Chord Symbols: i, ii°, III+, iv, V, VI, vii°, viii (i)

TYPE/QUALITY PATTERN of TRIADS in MAJOR and HARMONIC MINOR SCALES

Major and harmonic minor scales share the same Scale Degree Numbers and Technical Degree Names. The pattern of the Type/Quality of the Triads built on those Scale Degrees is different.

Scale Degree	Technical Scale Degree Name	Major Scale Functional Chord Symbol	Harmonic Minor Scale Functional Chord Symbol
$\hat{8}$	(Upper) Tonic	VIII (I) - Major	viii (i) - minor
$\hat{7}$	Leading Tone	vii° - diminished	vii° - diminished
$\hat{6}$	Submediant	vi - minor	VI - Major
$\hat{5}$	Dominant	V - Major	V - Major
$\hat{4}$	Subdominant	IV - Major	iv - minor
$\hat{3}$	Mediant	iii - minor	III+ - Augmented
$\hat{2}$	Supertonic	ii - minor	ii° - diminished
$\hat{1}$	(Lower) Tonic	I - Major	i - minor

At this level, triads will be built on the Major and the harmonic minor scales only.

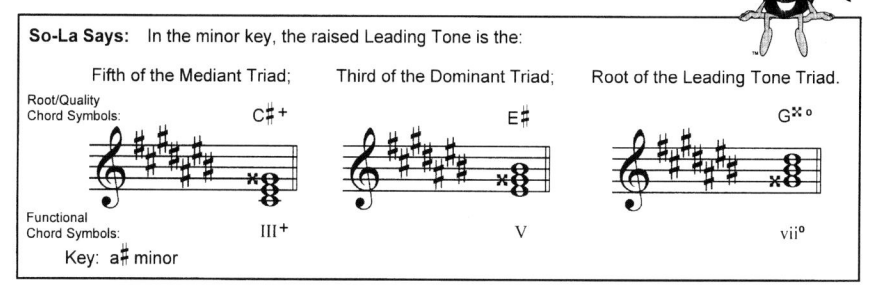

So-La Says: In the minor key, the raised Leading Tone is the:

Fifth of the Mediant Triad;   Third of the Dominant Triad;   Root of the Leading Tone Triad.

Root/Quality Chord Symbols: C#+   E#   G𝄪°

Functional Chord Symbols: III+   V   vii°

Key: a# minor

1. For each triad, name the minor key. Identify the root of each triad by its Scale Degree Name. Write the Root/Quality Chord Symbol above each triad and the Functional Chord Symbol below.

Root/Quality Chord Symbols: E#°   Bb   F#+   Bbm

Functional Chord Symbols: vii°   V   III+   iv

Scale Degree Name: Leading Tone   Dominant   Mediant   Subdominant

minor key: f# minor   eb minor   d# minor   f minor

♩ Ti-Do Time: Memorize the Type/Quality Pattern of Triads built on Major and harmonic minor scale degrees. Pop Quiz! Your Teacher will ask you to play and identify the Type/Quality of triads built on different Scale Degrees. Listen to the sound.

TRIAD POSITIONS and FUNCTIONAL CHORD SYMBOLS (FIGURED BASS)

Root/Quality Chord Symbols identify the Root, the Quality and the lowest note (the Slash = an inversion). The Root/Quality Chord Symbol is written above the triad.

Functional Chord Symbols identify the Root, the Quality and the Scale Degree. (The added Figured Bass indicates the Position of the triad.) The Functional Chord Symbol is written below the triad.

Root Position (root pos) Triad = The Root is the lowest note (the bottom note of the triad): V_3^5 or V.

First Inversion (1st inv) Triad = The Third is the lowest note (the bottom note of the triad): V_3^6 or V^6.

Second Inversion (2nd inv) Triad = The Fifth is the lowest note (the bottom note of the triad): V_4^6.

So-La Says: The Root/Quality Chord Symbol identifies the root, type/quality of the triad and the lowest note (which can be used to identify the position). A Slash Chord = 1st inv or 2nd inv.

The Functional Chord Symbol identifies the Scale Degree of the root (which can be used to identify the Major/minor key), the type/quality of the triad and the position.

Root/Quality Chord Symbols:	E♭+	D#o/F#	C/G
Functional Chord Symbols:	III+	vii°6	V_4^6
Root:	E♭ (Mediant)	D# (Leading Tone)	C (Dominant)
Type/Quality:	Augmented	diminished	Major
Position:	Root Position	1st inversion	2nd inversion
Key:	c minor	E Major	f minor

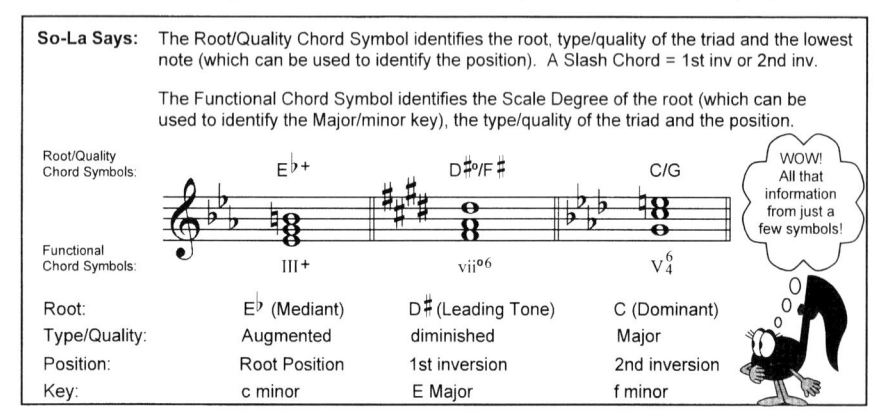

WOW! All that information from just a few symbols!

♪ **Ti-Do Tip:** At this level, it is preferable to use the "abbreviations" for the Figured Bass Numbers of the Functional Chord Symbols: Root Position = " " (no Figured Bass Numbers = Root Pos); and First Inversion = " 6 ". There is no abbreviation for Second Inversion.

1. a) Using the information in the Root/Quality Chord Symbol and the Functional Chord Symbol, identify the Root (and Scale Degree Name), Type/Quality, Position and minor key.
   b) Write each triad in solid/blocked form. Use a Key Signature and any necessary accidentals. Use whole notes.

Root/Quality Chord Symbol:	Gm/D	B/D#	E#o	F+/C#
Functional Chord Symbols:	i_4^6	V^6	vii°	$III+_4^6$
Root:	G (Tonic)	B (Dominant)	E# (Leading Tone)	F (Mediant)
Type/Quality:	minor	Major	diminished	Augmented
Position:	2nd inv	1st inv	root pos	2nd inv
Key:	g minor	e minor	f# minor	d minor

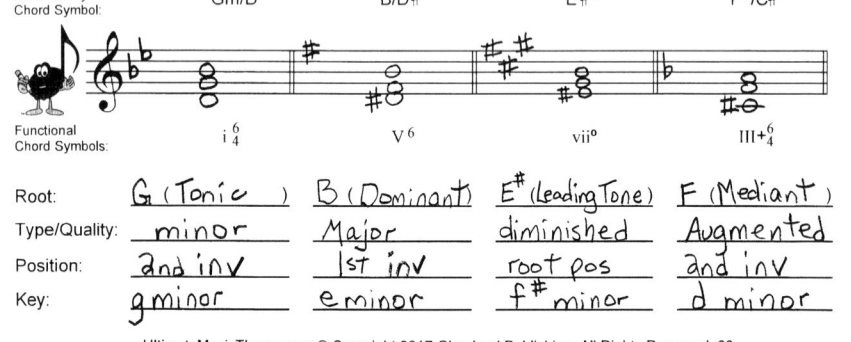

DOMINANT SEVENTH CHORDS - ROOT POSITION AND INVERSIONS

Review Pages 28 to 35 of the **Ultimate Music Theory LEVEL 6 Supplemental Workbook**: Dominant Seventh Chords.

Dominant Seventh Chord (**V7**) = 4 note chord built on the fifth degree of a scale.
Roman Numeral **V** = The Dominant Triad.
Number 7 after the Roman Numeral = The interval of a minor 7 above the Root of the Dominant Triad.
V7 = Root, Major 3, Perfect 5 and minor 7. These intervals are the same in both the Major and minor keys.

The **Type/Quality** of a Dominant Seventh Chord is simply Dominant 7th (Dom 7 or V7). In the **Root/Quality Chord Symbol**, this is indicated by adding the number "7" after the upper case letter name of the root note.

So-La Says: The Root/Quality Chord Symbol identifies the root, type/quality of the chord (7) and the lowest note (to identify the position). A Slash Chord = 1st inv, 2nd inv or 3rd inv.

The Functional Chord Symbol identifies the Scale Degree of the root (the Dominant of the Major/minor key) and the position.

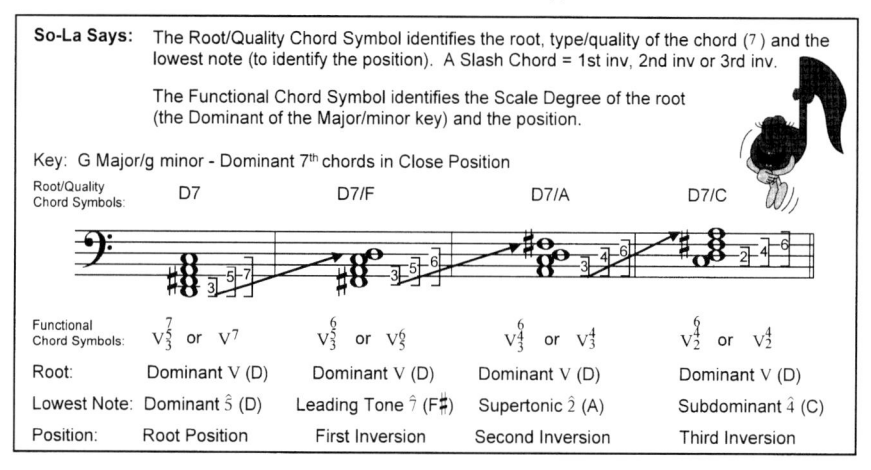

Key: G Major/g minor - Dominant 7th chords in Close Position

Root/Quality Chord Symbols:	D7	D7/F	D7/A	D7/C
Functional Chord Symbols:	V_3^7 or V^7	V_3^6 or V_5^6	V_3^6 or V_3^4	V_2^6 or V_2^4
Root:	Dominant V (D)	Dominant V (D)	Dominant V (D)	Dominant V (D)
Lowest Note:	Dominant $\hat{5}$ (D)	Leading Tone $\hat{7}$ (F♯)	Supertonic $\hat{2}$ (A)	Subdominant $\hat{4}$ (C)
Position:	Root Position	First Inversion	Second Inversion	Third Inversion

When written using accidentals, the Dominant Seventh Chord belongs to both the Major and Parallel (Tonic) minor keys. When written using a Key Signature, it belongs to either the Major or Parallel (Tonic) minor key.

♪ **Ti-Do Tip:** Use the "abbreviations" for the Figured Bass Numbers of the Functional Chord Symbols:
Root Position: V^7; First Inversion: V_5^6; Second Inversion: V_3^4; Third Inversion: V_2^4.

1. a) The following Dominant Seventh Chords are in the key of C Major and c minor. In each box on the staff, identify the interval number between the notes (2, 3, 4, 5, 6 or 7).
   b) Write the Root/Quality Chord Symbol above each chord and the Functional Chord Symbol below. Write both the full version and the abbreviation for each Functional Chord Symbol Figured Bass.

Root/Quality Chord Symbol: G7   G7/D   G7/B   G7/F

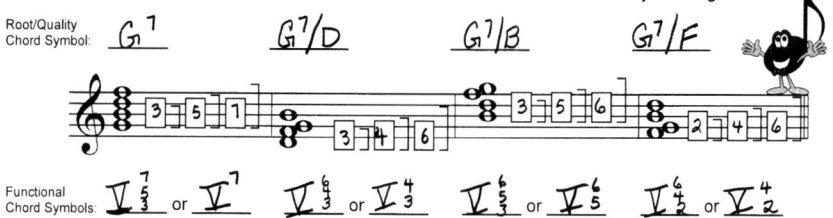

Functional Chord Symbols: V_3^7 or V^7 V_3^6 or V_3^4 V_3^6 or V_5^6 V_2^6 or V_2^4

NOTE PLACEMENT for DOMINANT SEVENTH CHORDS and INVERSIONS

The **3 Rules for Note Placement** when writing Inversions of Dominant Seventh Chords are:

Rule #1: In root position, the 4 notes are written on all lines or in all spaces.

Rule #2: In an inversion, the lower note in the interval of a 2nd (the lower hugging note) is always written on the left of the interval. (Interval of a 2nd - lower note on the left, upper note on the right.)

Rule #3: If a stem is added to make the notes half notes, there will be 3 notes on the correct side of the stem (according to the stem rule) and one note on the incorrect (opposite) side.

♩ **Ti-Do Tip**: Here are **3 Tips** to identify Correct or Incorrect note placements for Inversions of V7 Chords. Add a stem or "checking stem" in the direction of the note furthest away from the middle line: (A "checking stem" is a dotted line with a directional arrow at the top - up or bottom - down.)

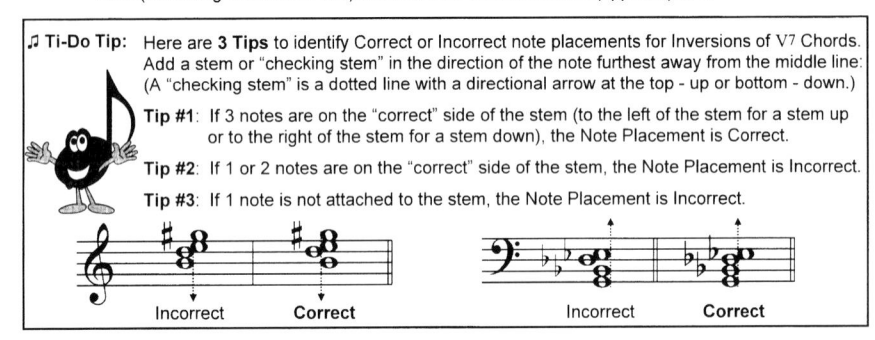

Tip #1: If 3 notes are on the "correct" side of the stem (to the left of the stem for a stem up or to the right of the stem for a stem down), the Note Placement is Correct.

Tip #2: If 1 or 2 notes are on the "correct" side of the stem, the Note Placement is Incorrect.

Tip #3: If 1 note is not attached to the stem, the Note Placement is Incorrect.

Incorrect **Correct**   Incorrect **Correct**

So-La Says: If checking the Note Placement using a "checking stem", the Correct Note Placement is:
Stem Up: 3 notes will be on the left of the stem and 1 note will be on the right.
Stem Down: 3 notes will be on the right of the stem and 1 note will be on the left.

1. Following the example in question i, for each Dominant Seventh Chord Inversion:
   a) In measures 1 and 2, use a stem or "checking stem" to check the Note Placement. Circle whether the Note Placement in each Dominant Seventh Chord is Correct or Incorrect.
   b) In measure 3, rewrite the correct Dominant Seventh Chord Inversion. Use whole notes. Write the Root/Quality Chord Symbol above and the Functional Chord Symbol below.

i) V7 of B♭ Major/b♭ minor in third inversion — F7/E♭ — V$_2^4$

ii) V7 of D Major/d minor in second inversion — A7/E — V$_3^4$

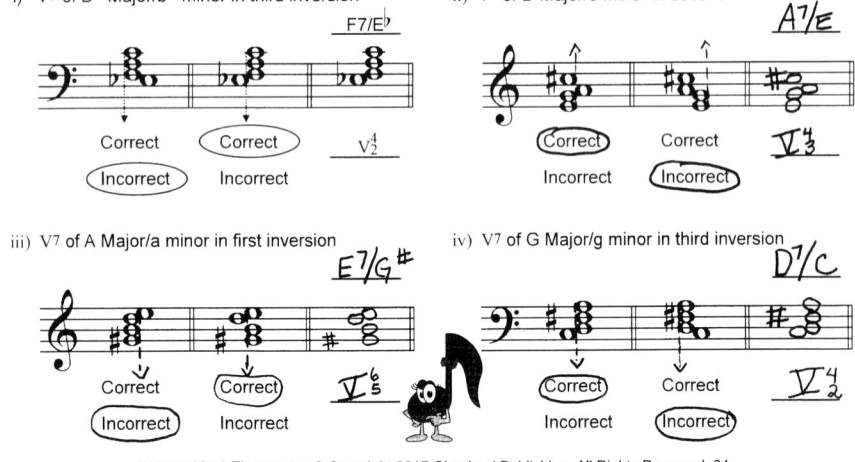

iii) V7 of A Major/a minor in first inversion — E7/G♯ — V$_5^6$

iv) V7 of G Major/g minor in third inversion — D7/C — V$_2^4$

ACCIDENTAL PLACEMENT for DOMINANT SEVENTH CHORDS and INVERSIONS

When written using **accidentals**, the Dominant Seventh Chord belongs to both the Major and Parallel (Tonic) minor keys. It is important to memorize the **Proper Placement of 2, 3 and 4 Accidentals**.

So-La Says: Observe the Proper Placement of Accidentals when writing Solid/Blocked V7 Chords.

Proper placement of **2 accidentals**:
1st accidental - written closer to the top note;
2nd accidental - written further away from the bottom note.

Proper placement of **3 accidentals**:
1st accidental - written closer to the top note;
2nd accidental - written further away from the bottom note;
3rd accidental - written furthest away from the middle note.

Proper placement of **4 accidentals**:
1st accidental - written closer to the top note;
2nd accidental - written further away from the bottom note;
3rd accidental - written further away from the 2nd highest note;
4th accidental - written furthest away from the 2nd lowest note.

♪ Ti-Do Tip: 2 Accidentals: [1/2]   3 Accidentals: [3 1/2]   4 Accidentals: [3 1/4 2]
(Top, Bottom)   (Top, Bottom, Middle)   (Top, Bottom, 2nd Highest, 2nd Lowest)

1. a) Add accidentals to create the following Dominant Seventh Chords (root position and inversions).
   b) Write the Root/Quality Chord Symbol above and the Functional Chord Symbol below.

   i) Dominant Seventh Chords of F# Major/f# minor.

   Root/Quality Chord Symbols: C#7   C#7/E#   C#7/G#   C#7/B

   Functional Chord Symbols: V7   V6/5   V4/3   V4/2

   ii) Dominant Seventh Chords of C# Major/c# minor.

   Root/Quality Chord Symbols: G#7   G#7/B#   G#7/D#   G#7/F#

   Functional Chord Symbols: V7   V6/5   V4/3   V4/2

WRITING DOMINANT SEVENTH CHORDS and INVERSIONS USING ACCIDENTALS

When writing inversions of a Dominant Seventh Chord, the placement of the **interval of a 2nd** is important.

So-La Says: Follow the **3 Steps for Note Placement** when writing an Inversion of a V7 Chord.

Step #1: Write the V7 in root position in square [I'm thinking] brackets on the right of the measure.

Step #2: Without using accidentals, write the lowest note of the inversion. Write the note that will be the highest note of the inversion. Determine the direction of the stem for the note that is the furthest away from the middle line (either the lowest or the highest note).

Step #3: Using the Stem Rule as your guide, add the remaining notes starting with the interval of the 2nd. The lower note of the "hugging notes" (interval of a 2nd) will be written to the left of the stem and will hug UP to the right. (If the lowest or highest note of the Chord is part of the interval of a 2nd, the note may have to be moved to the opposite side of the "stem".) Add any accidentals.

Example #1: Write the Dominant 7th Chord of G Major/g minor in 1st inversion. Use accidentals.

Step #1: Write in Root Position in square brackets.

Step #2: Write lowest and highest notes. Stems = up.

Step #3: Add the interval of a 2nd, with lower note on left. Add the remaining note and accidentals.

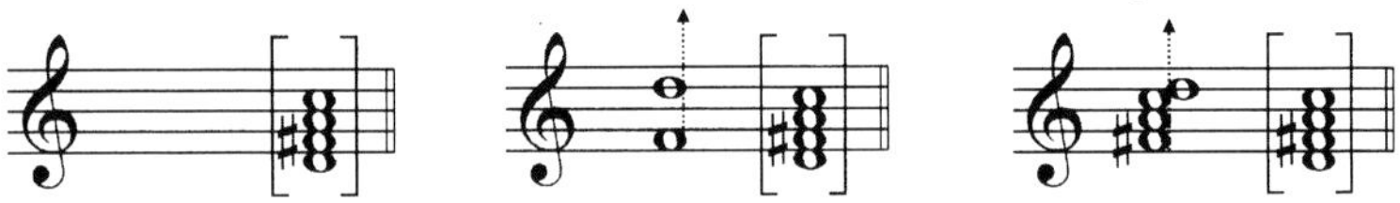

Example #2: Write the Dominant 7th Chord of G Major/g minor in 2nd inversion. Use accidentals.

Step #1: Write in Root Position in square brackets.

Step #2: Write lowest and highest notes. Stems = down.

Step #3: Add the interval of a 2nd, with lower note on left. Add the remaining note and accidentals.

♪ **Ti-Do Tip:** If "checking" your Note Placement by lightly adding a stem or "checking stem", be certain to **erase the stem** to complete writing the Chord using Whole Notes.

1. a) Write the following Dominant 7th Chords. Use whole notes. Use accidentals. (Write the V7 in root position in square [I'm thinking] brackets on the right of the measure first.)
   b) Write the Root/Quality Chord Symbol above each chord.

Root/Quality Chord Symbol: D7/C   E♭7/G   A7/E   C7/B♭

Functional Chord Symbols: V_2^4 of G Major/g minor V_5^6 of A♭ Major/a♭ minor V_3^4 of D Major/d minor V_2^4 of F Major/f minor

UltimateMusicTheory.com © Copyright 2017 Gloryland Publishing. All Rights Reserved.

WRITING DOMINANT SEVENTH CHORDS and INVERSIONS USING a KEY SIGNATURE

When written using a **Key Signature**, the Dominant Seventh Chord belongs to either the Major key or the Parallel (Tonic) minor key.

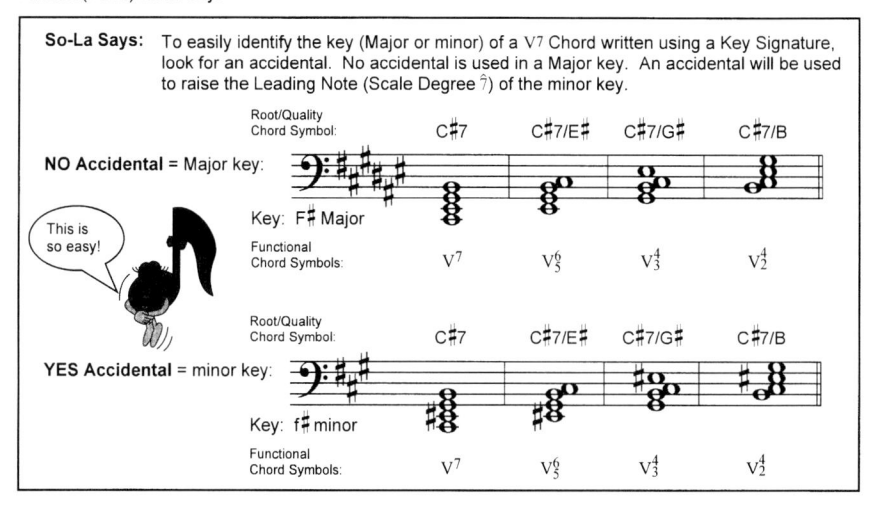

So-La Says: To easily identify the key (Major or minor) of a $V7$ Chord written using a Key Signature, look for an accidental. No accidental is used in a Major key. An accidental will be used to raise the Leading Note (Scale Degree $\hat{7}$) of the minor key.

NO Accidental = Major key:

Root/Quality Chord Symbol:	C#7	C#7/E#	C#7/G#	C#7/B

Key: F# Major

Functional Chord Symbols:	V^7	V^6_5	V^4_3	V^4_2

This is so easy!

YES Accidental = minor key:

Root/Quality Chord Symbol:	C#7	C#7/E#	C#7/G#	C#7/B

Key: f# minor

Functional Chord Symbols:	V^7	V^6_5	V^4_3	V^4_2

1. For each Dominant Seventh Chord, name the key to which it belongs. Write the Root/Quality Chord Symbol above and the Functional Chord Symbol below.

Root/Quality Chord Symbol:	Bb7/D♮	Bb7/D	A7/E	A7/E
Functional Chord Symbols:	V^6_5	V^6_5	V^4_3	V^4_3
Key:	eb minor	Eb Major	D Major	d minor

2. a) Write the following $V7$ Chords. Use whole notes. Use a Key Signature and any accidentals. (Write the $V7$ in root position in the square [I'm thinking] brackets on the right of the measure first.)
   b) Write the Root/Quality Chord Symbol above each chord.

Root/Quality Chord Symbol:	G7/B♮	F#7/C#	E7/G#	D7/C
Functional Chord Symbols:	V^6_5	V^4_3	V^6_5	V^4_2
	of c minor	of b minor	of A Major	of G Major

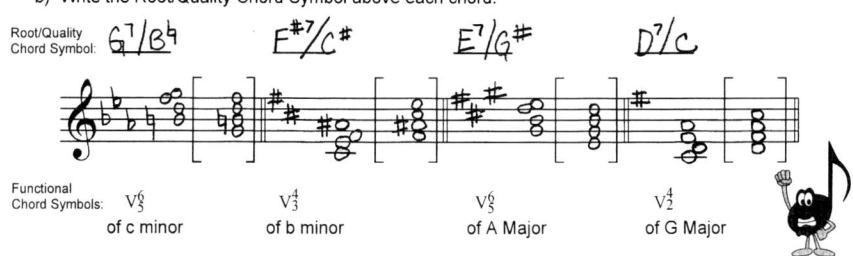

UltimateMusicTheory.com © Copyright 2017 Gloryland Publishing. All Rights Reserved.

LEADING-TONE DIMINISHED 7TH CHORDS - ACCIDENTALS

The Leading-Tone Diminished 7th Chord is a 4 note chord built on the raised seventh scale degree (↑$\hat{7}$) of the harmonic minor scale. It is also called the Diminished 7th Chord, the Leading-Note Diminished 7th Chord or simply the "seven diminished seven" Chord (vii°7).

The **Type/Quality** of a Diminished Seventh Chord is simply Diminished 7th (dim 7 or vii°7).

The **Root/Quality Chord Symbol** is indicated by adding the "°7" (or dim7) after the upper case letter name of the root note.

The **Functional Chord Symbol** is indicated by:
Roman Numeral **vii°** = The Leading Tone Triad (Type/Quality = diminished).
Number 7 after the Roman Numeral = The interval of a dim 7 above the Root of the Leading Tone Triad.
vii°7 = Root, minor 3, diminished 5 and diminished 7. (The distance between each note is a minor 3.)

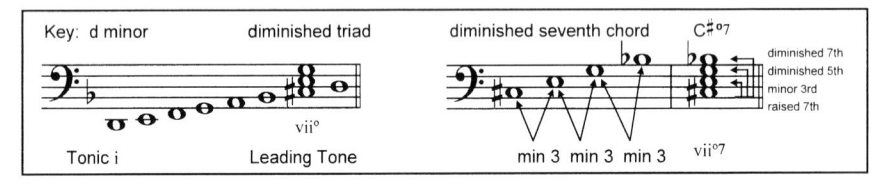

At this level, Leading-Tone Diminished 7th Chords will be written only in minor keys in Root Position.

So-La Says: Follow these 3 Steps to writing a Diminished Seventh Chord using Accidentals:

Write the Leading-Tone Diminished 7th Chord of g♯ minor. Use accidentals.

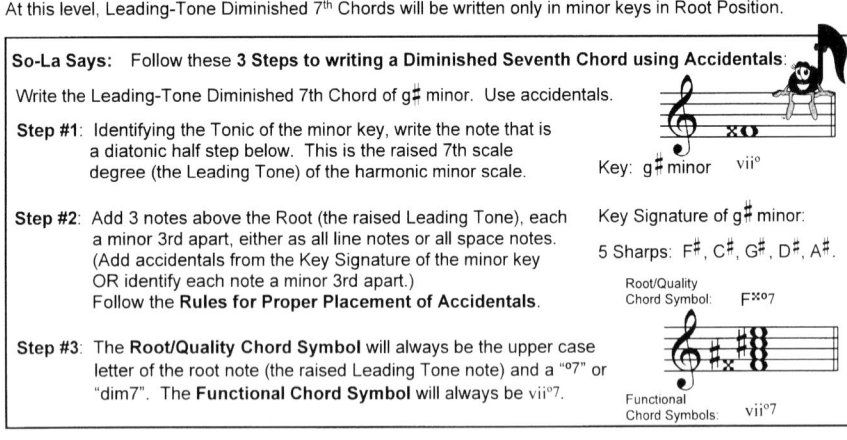

Step #1: Identifying the Tonic of the minor key, write the note that is a diatonic half step below. This is the raised 7th scale degree (the Leading Tone) of the harmonic minor scale.

Step #2: Add 3 notes above the Root (the raised Leading Tone), each a minor 3rd apart, either as all line notes or all space notes. (Add accidentals from the Key Signature of the minor key OR identify each note a minor 3rd apart.)
Follow the **Rules for Proper Placement of Accidentals**.

Key Signature of g♯ minor:
5 Sharps: F♯, C♯, G♯, D♯, A♯.

Root/Quality Chord Symbol: F𝄪°7

Step #3: The **Root/Quality Chord Symbol** will always be the upper case letter of the root note (the raised Leading Tone note) and a "°7" or "dim7". The **Functional Chord Symbol** will always be vii°7.

Functional Chord Symbols: vii°7

1. Write the following Leading-Tone Diminished 7th Chords. Use whole notes. Use accidentals.

Root/Quality Chord Symbol: D♯°7, E°7, G𝄪°7, A♯°7, A°7

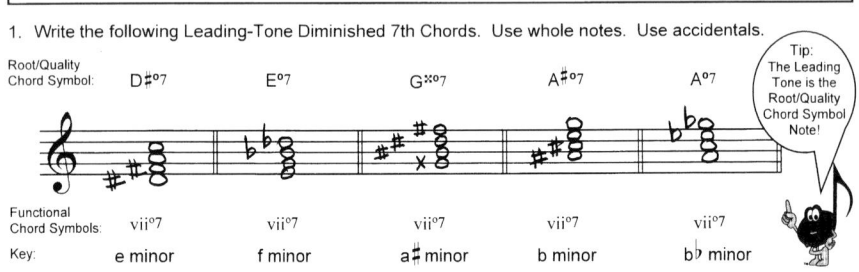

Functional Chord Symbols: vii°7, vii°7, vii°7, vii°7, vii°7
Key: e minor, f minor, a♯ minor, b minor, b♭ minor

Tip: The Leading Tone is the Root/Quality Chord Symbol Note!

LEADING-TONE DIMINISHED 7TH CHORDS - KEY SIGNATURE

At this level, Leading-Tone Diminished 7th Chords will be written only in Root Position in the **minor key**.

So-La Says: Follow these **3 Steps** to writing a Diminished Seventh Chord using a Key Signature:

Write the Leading-Tone Diminished 7th Chord of g# minor. Use a Key Signature.

Step #1: Write the Key Signature of the minor key. Write the raised 7th (↑$\hat{7}$) Scale Degree. Use an accidental. This note will be a diatonic half step below the Tonic of the harmonic minor key.

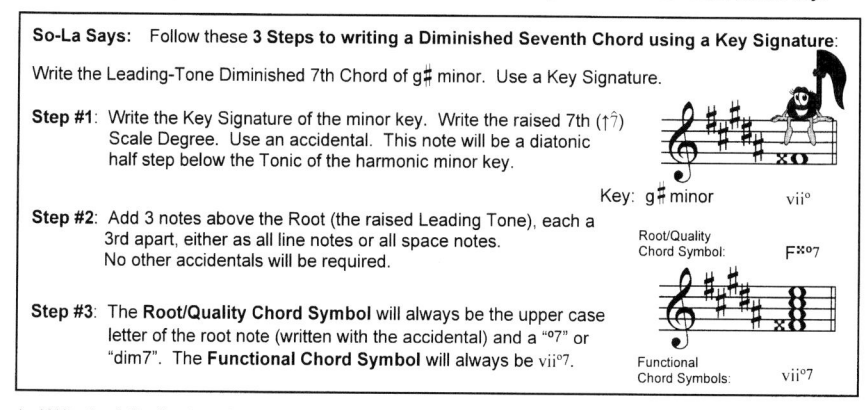

Key: g# minor   vii°

Step #2: Add 3 notes above the Root (the raised Leading Tone), each a 3rd apart, either as all line notes or all space notes. No other accidentals will be required.

Root/Quality Chord Symbol: F$^{\times 7}$

Step #3: The **Root/Quality Chord Symbol** will always be the upper case letter of the root note (written with the accidental) and a "°7" or "dim7". The **Functional Chord Symbol** will always be vii°7.

Functional Chord Symbols: vii°7

1. Write the following Leading-Tone Diminished 7th Chords. Use whole notes. Use a Key Signature.

Root/Quality Chord Symbol:	D#°7	E♭°7	G$^{\times 7}$	A#°7	A♮°7
Functional Chord Symbols:	vii°7	vii°7	vii°7	vii°7	vii°7
Key:	e minor	f minor	a# minor	b minor	b♭ minor

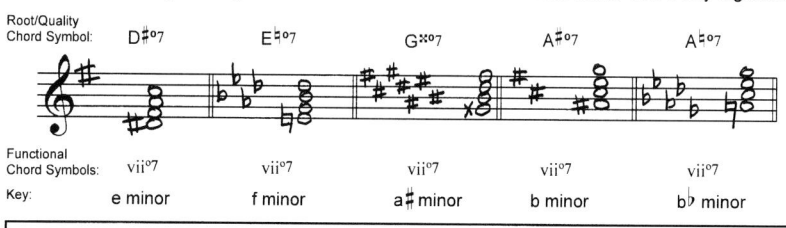

♪ Ti-Do Tip: To tell the difference between a Dominant 7th Chord and a Leading-Tone Diminished 7th Chord, here are **2 Easy Tips to Identify a V7 and a vii°7**:

Tip #1: In Root Position, the **interval between the Root and Third** is:
V7 Chord: Major 3;   vii°7 Chord: minor 3.

Tip #2: When written using a **Key Signature**, look for an accidental:
Major key V7 Chord: no accidental;
minor key V7 Chord: an accidental on the 3rd;
vii°7 Chord (always a minor key): an accidental on the Root.

C7   A7   C#°7

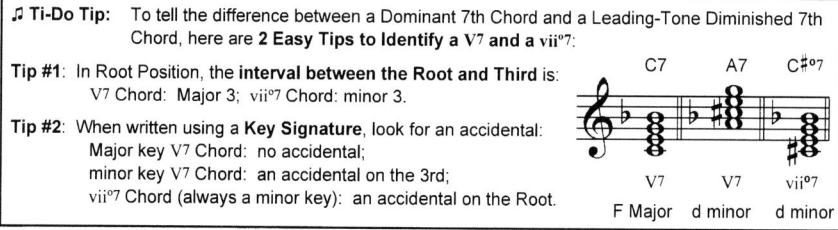

V7   V7   vii°7
F Major   d minor   d minor

2. Write the Root/Quality Chord Symbol above and the Functional Chord Symbol below. Name the key.

Root/Quality Chord Symbol:	G#°7	D7	D7	E(♮)°7	E7
Functional Chord Symbols:	vii°7	V7	V7	vii°7	V7
Key:	a minor	G Major	g minor	f minor	A Major

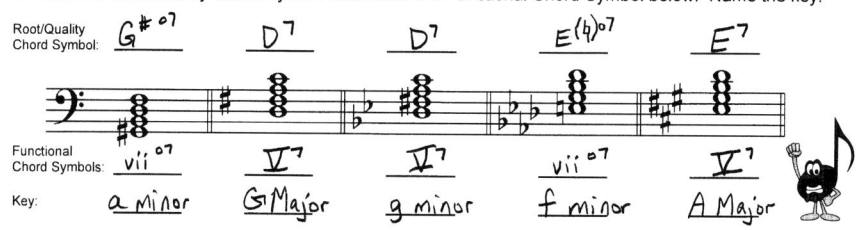

UltimateMusicTheory.com © Copyright 2017 Gloryland Publishing. All Rights Reserved.

OPEN to CLOSE POSITION CHORDS

Review Pages 29 to 34 of the **Ultimate Music Theory LEVEL 6 Supplemental Workbook**: Dominant Seventh Chords - Open and Close Position.

Close Position: Triad or Chord is written with notes as close together as possible.

Open Position: Triad or Chord is written "spread out", with intervals that can be larger than a 6th.

Staff Notation: Triad or Chord can be written in Open or Close Position on one staff or on the Grand Staff.

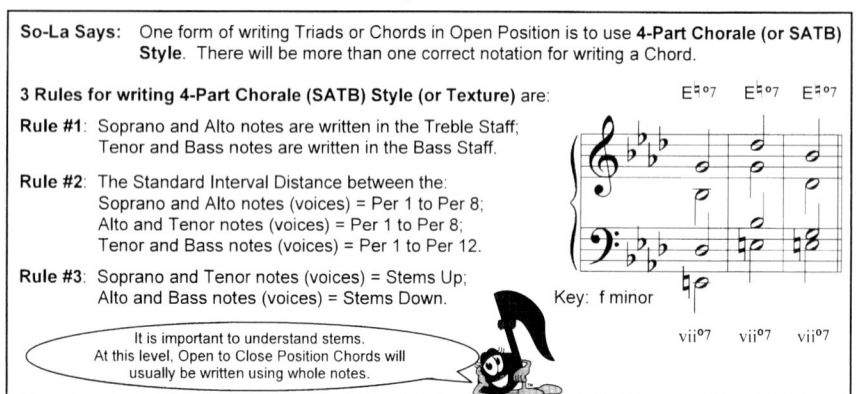

> **So-La Says**: One form of writing Triads or Chords in Open Position is to use **4-Part Chorale (or SATB) Style**. There will be more than one correct notation for writing a Chord.
>
> **3 Rules for writing 4-Part Chorale (SATB) Style (or Texture)** are:
>
> **Rule #1**: Soprano and Alto notes are written in the Treble Staff; Tenor and Bass notes are written in the Bass Staff.
>
> **Rule #2**: The Standard Interval Distance between the:
> Soprano and Alto notes (voices) = Per 1 to Per 8;
> Alto and Tenor notes (voices) = Per 1 to Per 8;
> Tenor and Bass notes (voices) = Per 1 to Per 12.
>
> **Rule #3**: Soprano and Tenor notes (voices) = Stems Up;
> Alto and Bass notes (voices) = Stems Down.
>
> *It is important to understand stems. At this level, Open to Close Position Chords will usually be written using whole notes.*

♪ **Ti-Do Tip**: When rewriting a Chord from Open Position to Close Position, the lowest note in the Bass Staff will remain the lowest note of the Chord (in root pos or in an inversion). However, the Close Position Chord can be rewritten at any pitch in either the Treble Staff or the Bass Staff.

1. Following the example in measure 1, rewrite each Open Position V7 or vii°7 Chord into Close Position. Write the Functional Chord Symbol V7 (or inversions) or vii°7 (root position only) below.

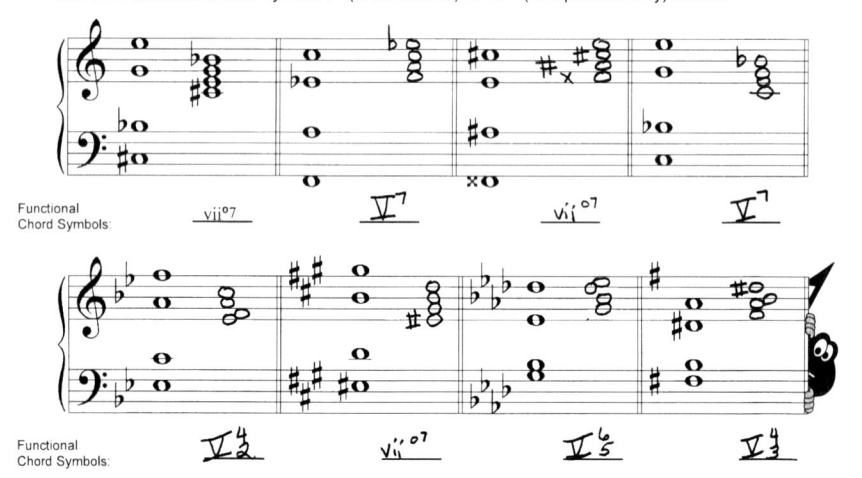

TRIAD and CHORD REVIEW

In Music, a Chord can be written with 3 notes or 4 notes (and even more).

Number of Notes	Scale Degrees	Type/Quality (and Intervals)
Triad - 3 notes: Root, Third, Fifth Or **Common Chord - 4 notes**: Root, Third, Fifth and one of the notes repeated.	Built on any degree of the Major or minor scale	Major (Maj): Root, Maj 3, Per 5 Minor (min): Root, min 3, Per 5 Augmented (Aug): Root, Maj 3, Aug. 5 Diminished (dim): Root, min 3, dim 5
Dominant 7th Chord - 4 notes: Root, Third, Fifth and Seventh	Built on Scale Degree $\hat{5}$ of the Major or harmonic minor scale	Dominant 7th (V7): Root, Maj 3, Per 5, min 7
Leading-Tone Diminished 7th Chord - 4 notes: Root, Third, Fifth and Seventh	Built on Scale Degree $\hat{7}$ of the harmonic minor scale	Diminished 7th (vii°7): Root, min 3, dim 5, dim 7

1. Write the following Solid/Blocked chords in the Treble Clef. Use the correct Key Signature and any necessary accidentals. Use whole notes.
   a) The Dominant 7th Chord of G Major in third inversion.
   b) The Mediant Triad of f minor harmonic form in first inversion.
   c) The Leading-Tone Diminished 7th Chord of b minor harmonic form in root position.
   d) The Submediant Triad of E Major in second inversion.

2. For each of the following Chords:
   a) Name the key.
   b) Name the Type of Chord.

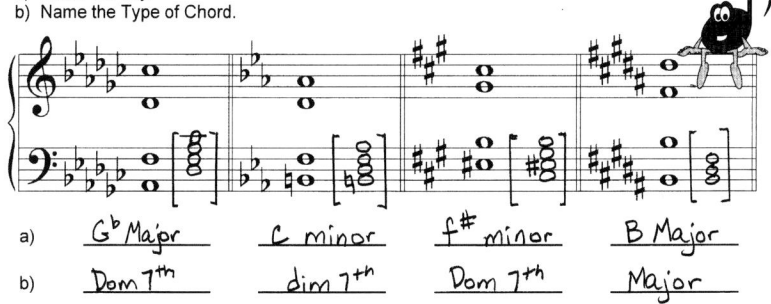

   a) G♭ Major   C minor   f♯ minor   B Major
   b) Dom 7th   dim 7th   Dom 7th   Major

3. Write the following Solid/Blocked Chords in the key of d minor. Use whole notes.

   Root/Quality Chord Symbol: A7/C♯   A/E   F+   C♯°7

   Functional Chord Symbols: V^6_5 V^6_4 III+   vii°7

CADENCE IDENTIFICATION

Review Pages 40 and 41 of the **Ultimate Music Theory LEVEL 6 Supplemental Workbook**: Authentic and Half Cadences; Cadence Identification.

Half Cadence (Imperfect Cadence): Major key: I - V or IV - V; minor key: i - V or iv - V.
A Half Cadence (HC) sounds unfinished, like a question at the end of a sentence.

Authentic Cadence (Perfect Cadence): Major key: V - I or V7 - I; minor key: V - i or V7 - i.
An Authentic Cadence sounds finished, like a period at the end of a sentence.

There are 2 types of Authentic Cadences:
  Perfect Authentic Cadence (PAC): The upper (Soprano) voice in the Tonic Chord is the Tonic note; both the Dominant and Tonic Chords are in Root Position.
  Imperfect Authentic Cadence (IAC): The upper (Soprano) voice is on the Mediant or Dominant rather than the Tonic note.

> **So-La Says:** **Keyboard Style Cadence**: Each Cadence chord is written in Close Position in the Treble Staff; the Root of each Cadence chord is written in the Bass Staff.
>
> **Voice Leading** is the movement between the voices or notes from one Cadence chord to the next.

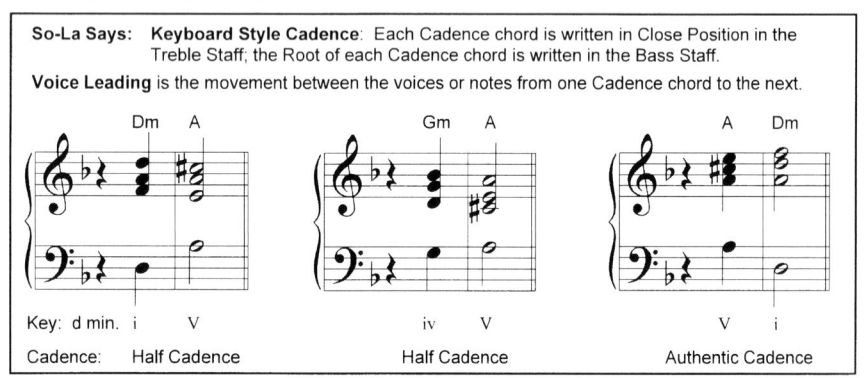

Key: d min.	i	V	iv	V	V	i
Cadence:	Half Cadence		Half Cadence		Authentic Cadence	

♪ **Ti-Do Tip:** When writing the Functional Chord Symbols for Cadences, each chord is in Root Position.
When writing the Root/Quality Chord Symbols for Cadences, each chord is in Root Position.

1. For each of the following cadences:
   a) Name the key (Major or minor).
   b) Write the Functional Chord Symbol below each chord and the Root/Quality Chord above.
   c) Name the type of Cadence (Authentic or Half).

Root/Quality Chord Symbol: Cm   G   G   A   G#   C#m

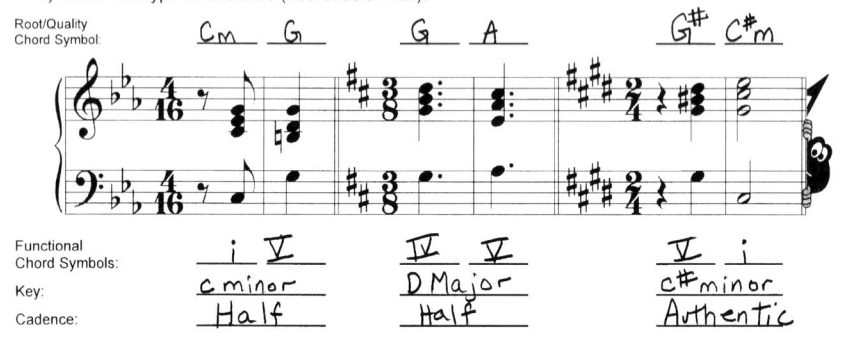

Functional Chord Symbols: i   V   IV   V   V   i
Key: c minor   D Major   c# minor
Cadence: Half   Half   Authentic

DOMINANT SEVENTH to TONIC AUTHENTIC CADENCE IDENTIFICATION

An Authentic Cadence written from the Dominant Seventh Chord to the Tonic Chord can be written 2 ways:
Complete Dominant Seventh Chord to **Incomplete** Tonic Chord;
Incomplete Dominant Seventh Chord to **Complete** Tonic Chord.

So-La Says: When writing a **Keyboard Style Cadence**, it is better to use the Incomplete Dominant Seventh Chord to Complete Tonic Chord Progression.

In an Incomplete V7 Chord to Complete I/i Chord, the Incomplete V7 Chord is written with a doubled Dominant ($\hat{5}$), single Leading Tone ($\hat{7}$) and single Subdominant ($\hat{4}$). The Supertonic ($\hat{2}$) note is omitted.

Incomplete V7 Chord: Treble Staff - Dominant ($\hat{5}$), Leading Tone ($\hat{7}$), Subdominant ($\hat{4}$);
Bass Staff - Dominant ($\hat{5}$).
Complete I/i Chord: Treble Staff - Tonic ($\hat{1}$), Mediant ($\hat{3}$), Dominant ($\hat{5}$);
Bass Staff - Tonic ($\hat{1}$).

The best **Voice Leading** in an Incomplete V7 Chord is to use the hugging notes (interval of a second) between the Subdominant ($\hat{4}$) and the Dominant ($\hat{5}$). The Dominant ($\hat{5}$) will be the Common Note (the note in the same voice in both chords), the Subdominant ($\hat{4}$) will fall (step down) to the Mediant ($\hat{3}$).

♪ **Ti-Do Tip:** At this level, students will write Cadences only in **Keyboard Style**.
In Level 8, students will learn how to write Cadences in **Chorale (SATB) Style**.

1. For each of the following cadences:
   a) Name the key (Major or minor).
   b) Write the Functional Chord Symbol below each chord and the Root/Quality Chord above.
   c) Name the type of Cadence (Authentic or Half).

Root/Quality Chord Symbol: $D^{\#7}$ $G^{\#}m$ F^7 B^b A^{b7} D^b

Functional Chord Symbols: V^7 i V^7 I V^7 I
Key: g# minor   Bb Major   Db Major
Cadence: Authentic   Authentic   Authentic

HALF CADENCE VOICE LEADING

Keyboard Style Cadence: the 3 notes in the Close Position Triads in the Treble Staff are called Soprano (upper) voice, Alto (middle) voice and Tenor (lower) voice. The note in the Bass Staff is the Bass voice.

Voice Leading refers to how voices move from one chord to another. In good voice leading, each voice moves as smoothly as possible from one chord note to another. For ease of singing, the voice leading between chord notes is by repeated note (same/unison), by step (2nd up/down) or by skip (3rd up/down).

The purpose of **Voice Leading**, the movement between the voices/notes from one Cadence chord to the next, is to keep a "**consonant**" (pleasant or agreeable) sound as the cadence resolves.

"**Dissonant**" intervals cause tension and a musical desire to resolve to a consonant interval. Voice Leading for the Bass voice notes should move in **contrary motion** to the voices in the Treble Staff. (Review Pages 46 and 55 of the UMT LEVEL 6 Supplemental Workbook: Cadences & Voice Leading.)

So-La Says: In a Half Cadence, the voices in the first chord in the Treble Staff (I/i or IV/iv) can be written in any position, however the voices must resolve correctly (move in the proper way) to the second chord (V).

Cadence	Chord Progression	Triad Scale Degrees	Half Cadence Voice Leading	
Half Cadence	Major: I - V Minor: i - V	I/i (Tonic): $\hat{1}, \hat{3}, \hat{5}$ ($\hat{1}$ in Bass) to V (Dominant): $\hat{5}, \hat{7}, \hat{2}$ ($\hat{5}$ in Bass)	$\hat{5} \rightarrow \hat{5}$ $\hat{3} \searrow \hat{2}$ $\hat{1} \searrow \hat{7}$ Bass to ascend $\hat{1} \nearrow \hat{5}$	or $\hat{5} \nearrow \hat{7}$ $\hat{3} \nearrow \hat{5}$ $\hat{1} \nearrow \hat{2}$ Bass to descend $\hat{1} \searrow \hat{5}$
Half Cadence	Major: IV - V Minor: iv - V	IV/iv (Subdominant): $\hat{4}, \hat{6}, \hat{1}\,(\hat{8})$ ($\hat{4}$ in Bass) to V (Dominant): $\hat{5}, \hat{7}, \hat{2}$ ($\hat{5}$ in Bass)	$\hat{1} \searrow \hat{7}$ $\hat{6} \searrow \hat{5}$ $\hat{4} \searrow \hat{2}$ Bass to ascend $\hat{4} \nearrow \hat{5}$	

When progressing from I/i to V, do not mix the voice leading. Keep the common note (then descend in the other 2 Treble Staff voices) OR do not keep the common note (and all 3 voices ascend in the Treble Staff).

1. Complete the following Half Cadences in the key of f minor. F G A♭ B♭ C D♭ E♮ F
   $\hat{1}$ $\hat{2}$ $\hat{3}$ $\hat{4}$ $\hat{5}$ $\hat{6}$ $\hat{7}$ $\hat{8}\,(\hat{1})$
   a) Write the Scale Degree Number for the Soprano (upper) voices above each chord.
   b) Add notes below the given Soprano (upper) voices. Add the Bass voice notes (moving in Contrary Motion). Use the appropriate note values and any necessary accidentals.
   c) Write the Functional Chord Symbol below each chord.

Soprano Voice Scale Degrees: $\hat{3}$ $\hat{2}$ $\hat{4}$ $\hat{2}$ $\hat{3}$ $\hat{5}$

Functional Chord Symbols: i   V   iv   V   i   V

AUTHENTIC CADENCE VOICE LEADING

A **Tendency Tone** is an "active" scale degree that tends to resolve (move) by step to a less active scale degree (usually to notes of the Tonic Triad). The Dominant Seventh Chord contains two Tendency Tones.

Tendency Tone #1: The Leading Tone, the 3rd note of the Dominant 7th Chord
(Scale Degree $\hat{7}$). In the language of harmony, this Tone is called the "3rd of V7".

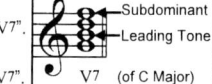

Tendency Tone #2: The Subdominant, the 7th note of the Dominant 7th Chord
(Scale Degree $\hat{4}$). In the language of harmony, this Tone is called the "7th of V7".

Observe the **3 Tendency Tone Rules**:

Rule #1: When the **Leading Tone** is in the **Soprano** (upper) voice in the Treble Staff V or V7 Chord, it must resolve (move) by a step up to the Tonic (Degree $\hat{1}$ in the Tonic Chord): $\hat{7} \nearrow \hat{1}$.

Rule #2: When the **Leading Tone** is in the **Alto** (middle) or the **Tenor** (lower) voice in the Treble, it may resolve to the Tonic (Degree $\hat{1}$ in the Tonic Chord) or the Dominant (Degree $\hat{5}$): $\hat{7} \nearrow \hat{1}$ or $\hat{7} \searrow \hat{5}$.

Rule #3: In V7 - I/i, the "**7th of the Dominant 7th Chord**" (Scale Degree $\hat{4}$, Subdominant) must step down to the Mediant (Scale Degree $\hat{3}$ in the Tonic Chord): $\hat{4} \searrow \hat{3}$. Avoid writing it in the Soprano voice.

So-La Says:	In an Authentic Cadence, the voices in the first chord in the Treble Staff (V or V7) can be written in different positions as long as the **Tendency Tone Rules** are observed.		
Cadence	Chord Progression	Triad Scale Degrees	Authentic Cadence Voice Leading
Authentic Cadence	Major: V - I Minor: V - i	V (Dominant): $\hat{5}, \hat{7}, \hat{2}$ to I/i (Tonic): $\hat{1}, \hat{3}, \hat{5}$	$\hat{2} \nearrow \hat{3}$ or $\hat{2} \searrow \hat{1}$ $\hat{7} \nearrow \hat{1}$ $\hat{7} \searrow \hat{5}$ (not in Soprano) $\hat{5} \rightarrow \hat{5}$ $\hat{5} \searrow \hat{3}$ Bass to descend Bass to ascend $\hat{5} \searrow \hat{1}$ $\hat{5} \nearrow \hat{1}$
Authentic Cadence	Major: V7 - I Minor: V7 - i	V7 (Incomplete Dominant Seventh): $\hat{5}, \hat{7}, \hat{4}$ ($\hat{5}$ in Bass, omit the $\hat{2}$) to I/i (Complete Tonic): $\hat{1}, \hat{3}, \hat{5}$ ($\hat{1}$ in Bass)	$\hat{4} \searrow \hat{3}$ (Avoid writing in Soprano voice) $\hat{7} \nearrow \hat{1}$ $\hat{5} \rightarrow \hat{5}$ Bass to ascend OR Bass to descend $\hat{5} \nearrow \hat{1}$ $\hat{5} \searrow \hat{1}$

1. Following the example in the first cadence, on the lines beside each Authentic Cadence, write the Scale Degree Numbers for each chord to show the Voice Leading. Use arrows to indicate each direction (up $\nearrow$; down $\searrow$; or common note $\rightarrow$).

First example — Key: f# minor, V7 i
Voice Leading:
$\hat{5} \rightarrow \hat{5}$
$\hat{4} \searrow \hat{3}$
$\hat{7} \nearrow \hat{1}$
$\hat{5} \nearrow \hat{1}$

Second example — Key: a minor, V7 i
Voice Leading:
$\hat{7} \nearrow \hat{1}$
$\hat{5} \rightarrow \hat{5}$
$\hat{4} \searrow \hat{3}$
$\hat{5} \searrow \hat{1}$

Third example — Key: F Major, V I
Voice Leading:
$\hat{5} \searrow \hat{3}$
$\hat{2} \searrow \hat{1}$
$\hat{7} \searrow \hat{5}$
$\hat{5} \nearrow \hat{1}$

STEPS to WRITING CADENCES at PHRASE ENDINGS

In melody writing, a cadence at the end of each phrase is like punctuation at the end of each sentence.

A Half Cadence (Major key: I - V or IV - V; minor key: i - V or iv - V) sounds unfinished, providing a brief pause in the music, like a comma or question mark. It is usually used at the end of the first phrase.

An Authentic Cadence (Major key: V - I or V7 - I; minor key: V - i or V7 - i) sounds finished, like a period at the end of a sentence. It is usually used at the end of the second phrase (or at the end of the melody).

So-La Says: To select which Cadence to use at the end of each phrase, look at the Voice Leading (the Scale Degrees used) in the Soprano melody notes.

Soprano Melody Note (Scale Degree found in Chord)	$\hat{1}$ Tonic	$\hat{2}$ Supertonic	$\hat{3}$ Mediant	$\hat{4}$ Subdominant	$\hat{5}$ Dominant	$\hat{6}$ Submediant	$\hat{7}$ Leading Tone
Major key Chords	I or IV	V	I	IV or V7	I, V or V7	IV	V or V7
Minor key Chords (Use Harmonic Minor - raise the Leading Tone)	i or iv	V	i	iv or V7	i, V or V7	iv	V or V7

Follow these **3 Steps to Write a Cadence at the end of a Phrase**:

Step #1: Identify the key of the melody.

Step #2: Identify the Scale Degrees of the final 2 notes in the phrase. Determine which chord each note belongs to (I/i, IV/iv, V or V7), then determine the appropriate cadence type (Half or Authentic).

Step #3: Write the remaining chord notes below the given Soprano voice (in the Treble Staff) using smooth (consonant) Voice Leading. Write the root note of each chord in the Bass Staff (moving in contrary motion).

♩ **Ti-Do Tip**: To easily determine what Chords and Cadences to use, create a Chord Chart (on your UMT Whiteboard or at the beginning of your melody). Write the notes (letters) of the Dominant (7th) Chord (writing the "7" note in brackets), the Subdominant Chord and the Tonic Chord.

1. Write a Cadence at the end of each phrase.
    a) Name the key. Complete the Chord Chart with the notes (letter names) for each Chord (write the 7 of the Dominant Seventh Chord in the bracket).
    b) Write the Soprano Voice Scale Degree Number above the final 2 notes in each phrase. Write the Functional Chord Symbols and the Cadence Type below.
    c) Add the remaining notes (in both the Treble and Bass) to complete each Cadence.

WRITING KEYBOARD STYLE CADENCES at PHRASE ENDINGS

So-La Says: The **3 Rules** for writing Cadence Chords in Keyboard Style are:

Rule #1: For each Chord, 3 notes are written in the Treble Staff in Close Position and 1 note (the root) is written in the Bass Staff.

Rule #2: The Standard Interval Distance between the lowest note in the Treble and the Bass note (the vertical or "harmonic" distance) is a 12th or less.

Rule #3: All notes follow the Stem Rule. All notes in each Cadence Chord will use the same note values.

1. Write a Cadence at the end of each phrase. There may be more than one correct Cadence.
   a) Name the key. Complete the Chord Chart with the notes for each Chord (write the 7 of the Dominant Seventh Chord in the bracket).
   b) Write the Soprano Voice Scale Degree Number above the final 2 notes in each phrase. Write the Functional Chord Symbols and the Cadence Type below.
   c) Add the remaining notes (in both the Treble and Bass) to complete each Cadence.

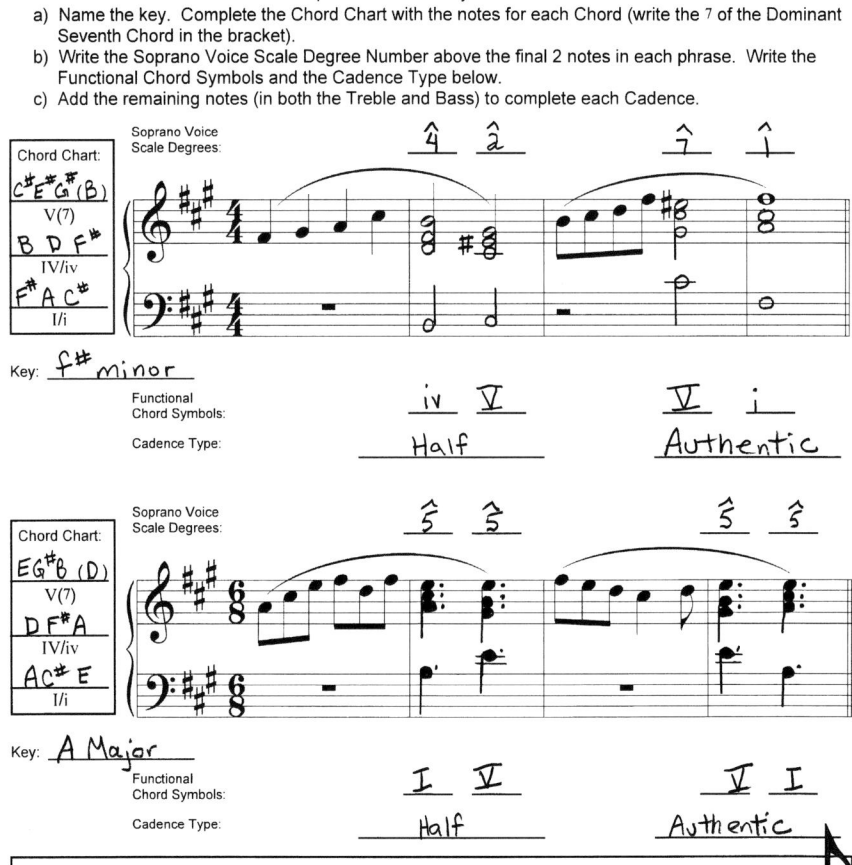

Ti-Do Time: Play the melodies (with the cadences) on your instrument. Listen to the smooth (consonant) motion between the voices at each cadence.

NEW "PERFORMANCE" TERMS

"**Performance**" **Terms** in music can be used to describe the style of performance or the musical character to be portrayed when performing.

Performance Term	Definition (Musical Direction)
agitato	agitated (feeling or sounding nervous)
dolente	sad
giocoso	humorous, jocose (playful)
martellato	strongly accented, hammered
mesto	sad, mournful
morendo	dying, fading away (gradually get softer and slower)
pesante	weighty, with emphasis (heavy and ponderous)
risoluto	resolute (purposeful, determined, with resolve)
scherzando	playful (in a playful manner)
semplice	simple (to play simply)
sonore	sonorous (imposingly deep and full)
sostenuto	sustained (played in a prolonged manner)
sotto voce	soft, subdued, under the breath
vivo	lively

♪ **Ti-Do Tip:** These **Performance Terms** are often written by the Composer to provide the performer with direction as to how the music is to be interpreted.

So-La Says: Review the Musical Terms, Definitions and Signs in the Intermediate Rudiments Workbook and in the LEVEL 6 Supplemental Workbook:

Articulation, Signs, Terms, Tempo, Changes in Tempo, Dynamics and Stylistic (Style in Performance).

1. Two or more Italian Terms can be used together, joined by the term for "and" (*e*, *ed*). Explain the meaning of the Italian Terms below.

   a) *dolente ed sostenuto*   _Sad and sustained_

   b) *mesto e morendo*   _sad, mournful and dying fading away (gradually get softer and slower)_

   c) *martellato ed agitato*   _strongly accented, hammered and agitated_

   d) *giocoso e vivo*   _humorous and lively_

   e) *sonore ed risoluto*   _sonorous and resolute_

   f) *semplice ed sotto voce*   _simple and soft, subdued, under the breath_

ANALYSIS and TERMS

Italian Terms relating to performance instruction include:

tacet - be silent

tutti - a passage for the ensemble (to all play together, at the same time)

volti subito (*v.s.*) - turn the page quickly

So-La Says:	Signs in music can be written to indicate specific direction.
	glissando, gliss. - Continuous slide upward (↗) between 2 or more pitches.
	glissando, gliss. - Continuous slide downward (↘) between 2 or more pitches.
8va ⌐	*ottava alta* - play the notes under this sign one octave higher.
8vb ⌐	*ottava bassa* - play the notes above this sign one octave lower.
15ma ⌐	*quindicesima alta* - play the notes under this sign two octaves higher.
15ba ⌐	*quindicesima bassa* - play the notes above this sign two octaves lower.

"**Volta Brackets**", also called "first ending" and "second ending", are used when a performer is to play a section the first time it is reached, and, after repeating, plays the second section (or ending).

Notice that the "end repeat" is written after the 1st ending. A double bar line is used to separate the 2nd ending from the measures that follow.

♪ **Ti-Do Tip:** *volta* - time (for example, *prima volta* = first time; *seconda volta* = second time)

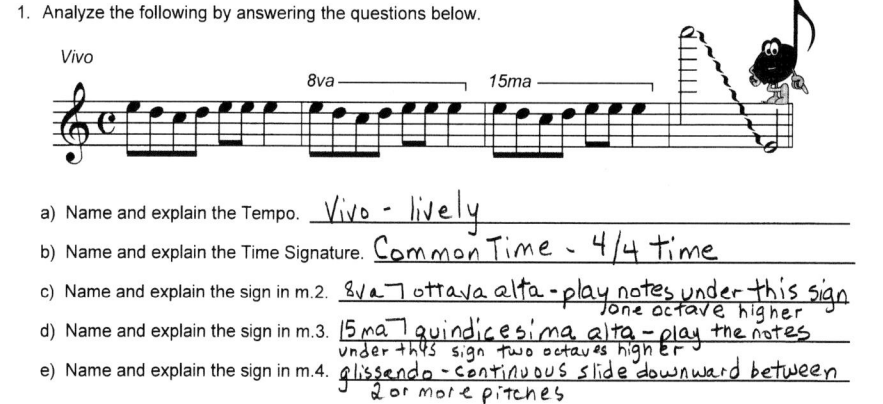

1. Analyze the following by answering the questions below.

   Vivo

   a) Name and explain the Tempo. __Vivo - lively__
   b) Name and explain the Time Signature. __Common Time - 4/4 time__
   c) Name and explain the sign in m.2. __8va ⌐ ottava alta - play notes under this sign one octave higher__
   d) Name and explain the sign in m.3. __15ma ⌐ quindicesima alta - play the notes under this sign two octaves higher__
   e) Name and explain the sign in m.4. __glissando - continuous slide downward between 2 or more pitches__

MELODY ANALYSIS - NON-CHORD TONES

A melody is a combination of melodic shape (movement of pitch) and rhythmic variety (duration of pitch). A melody can move by step, skip, leap or repeated note. A melody may move directly from one chord tone to another or move by step into a non-chord tone followed by a step into the same or new chord tone.

A **Non-Chord Tone**, or non-harmonic note, is a note that does not belong to the chord (harmony).

So-La Says: Non-Chord Tone (a step between 2 chord tones) may be a passing tone or a neighbor tone. An "unaccented" Non-Chord Tone falls on a weak beat or weak part (subdivision) of a beat.

A **passing tone** "pt" is a non-chord tone moving by step (same direction), as a bridge connecting two chord tones.

A **neighbor tone** "nt" is a non-chord tone moving by step (up or down), as a bump adjacent to a returning chord tone.

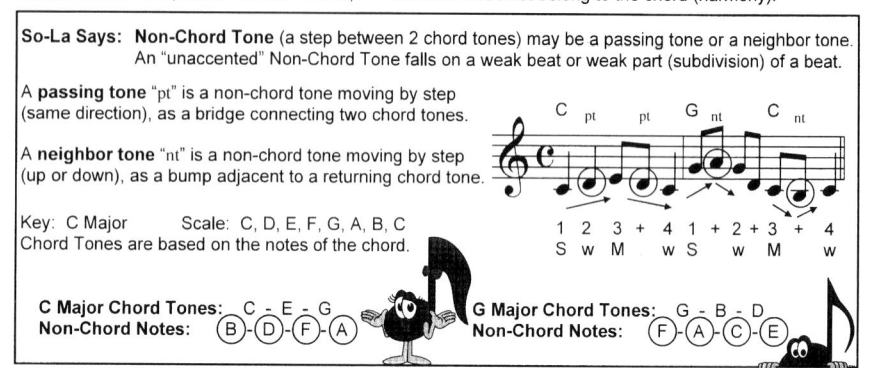

Key: C Major   Scale: C, D, E, F, G, A, B, C
Chord Tones are based on the notes of the chord.

C Major Chord Tones: C - E - G
Non-Chord Notes: B - D - F - A

G Major Chord Tones: G - B - D
Non-Chord Notes: F - A - C - E

♩ **Ti-Do Tip:** Passing tone "pt" bridge - SAME direction. Neighbor tone "nt" bump - UP or DOWN direction.

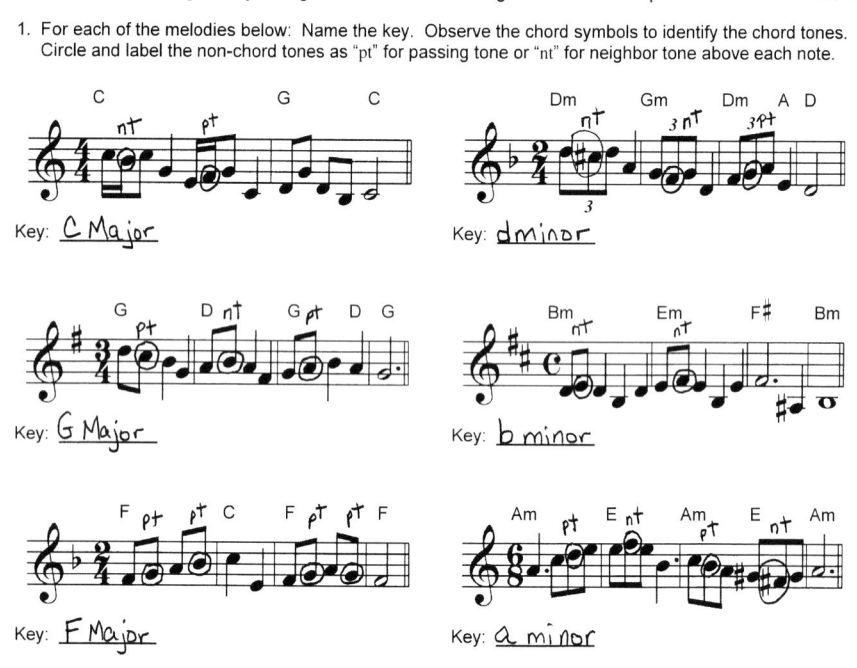

1. For each of the melodies below: Name the key. Observe the chord symbols to identify the chord tones. Circle and label the non-chord tones as "pt" for passing tone or "nt" for neighbor tone above each note.

Key: C Major

Key: d minor

Key: G Major

Key: b minor

Key: F Major

Key: a minor

MELODY WRITING - NON-CHORD TONES and FUNCTIONAL CHORD SYMBOLS

A melody often uses chord tones as a framework around which to "weave" non-chord tones as "melodic decoration". Non-chord tones are notes that do not belong to the chord/triad used in the harmony.

The Tonic triad (I, i) chord tones are: $\hat{1}, \hat{3}, \hat{5}$. A melody based on the Tonic triad may use any combination of scale degrees $\hat{2}, \hat{4}, \hat{6}$ or $\hat{7}$ (non-chord notes) as melodic decoration.

So-La Says: **Functional Chord Symbols** identify the implied Chord Tones upon which a melody is based. Unaccented Non-Chord Tones fall on weak beats or on weak subdivisions of beats.

Functional Chord Symbols		Chord Tones	Non-Chord Tones
Tonic Chord	I, i	$\hat{1}, \hat{3}, \hat{5}$	$\hat{2}, \hat{4}, \hat{6}, \hat{7}$
Subdominant	IV, iv	$\hat{4}, \hat{6}, \hat{8}$	$\hat{2}, \hat{3}, \hat{5}, \hat{7}$
Dominant (7th)	V, (V7)	$\hat{5}, \hat{7}, \hat{2}, (\hat{4})$	$\hat{1}, \hat{3}, \hat{6}$

For analysis of Treble Staff Melodies (without a Bass voice), **Root/Quality Chord Symbols** are written as **Root Position**.

Key: G Major I   V   I
Chord tones G, B, D   Chord tones D, F♯, A
I - Non-chord tone A   V - Non-chord tone B

A passing tone "pt" is a non-chord tone in between two different chord tones a third apart.

A neighbor tone "nt" is a non-chord tone, one step higher or lower, in between two identical chord tones.

♪ **Ti-Do Tip:** Non-chord tone: a decorative passing tone "pt" or neighbor tone "nt" (or auxiliary note).

1. Name the key. Observe the Functional Chord Symbols to identify chord tones. Write the Root/Quality Chord Symbol (as root position) above the measure. Circle and label the non-chord tones as "pt" or "nt".

Em pt   Am nt   Em pt   B nt

Key: **e minor**   i   iv   i   V

2. For each of the melodies below: Name the key. Write the Root/Quality Chord Symbol (as root position) above each measure. Add the missing notes below the bracket to complete each measure. Use non-chord tones. Circle and label the non-chord tones as "pt" for passing tone or "nt" for neighbor tone.

B♭ pt   E♭ nt   B♭ pt   pt F pt

Key: **B♭ Major**   I   IV (or D)   I   V

Cm nt   Fm nt   G nt   Cm nt

Key: **C minor**   i (or D)   iv (or E♭)   V (or C)   i (or B♮)

* nt may move up or down between chord tones. (nt one possible answer)

MELODY WRITING - ADDING MELODIC DECORATION - PASSING TONES and NEIGHBOR TONES

When writing a melody, the harmonic line outlining the simple progression of chords can be made more interesting by using different techniques. "Melodic Decoration" is adding non-chord tones such as a decorative passing tone "pt" or neighbor tone "nt" (auxiliary note) to embellish the basic melody.

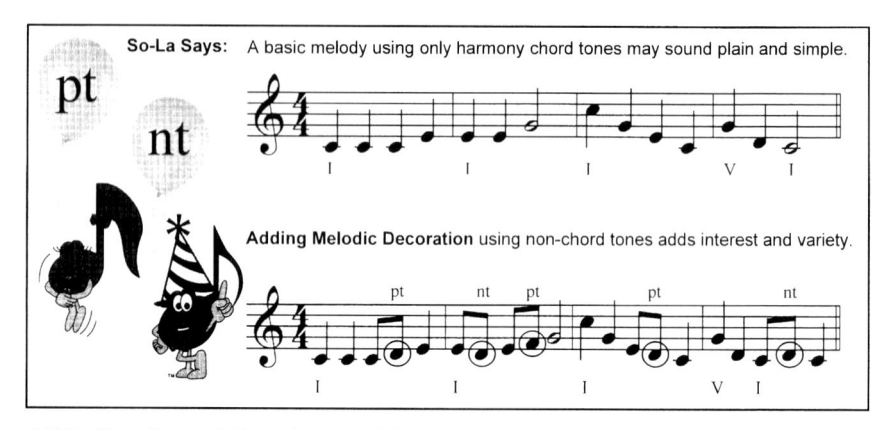

So-La Says: A basic melody using only harmony chord tones may sound plain and simple.

Adding Melodic Decoration using non-chord tones adds interest and variety.

♪ **Ti-Do Tip:** Unaccented non-chord tones fall on the weak beat or weak subdivision of the beat. When adding neighbor tones, there will be more than one correct answer (above or below).

1. For each of the following melodies: a) Name the key. b) Rewrite each melody adding melodic decoration using (unaccented) non-chord tones. c) Circle and label the non-chord tones as "pt" or "nt".
   (one possible answer for each below)

i) Key: F Major

ii) Key: e minor

COMPOSING - USING CHORD TONES and NON-CHORD TONES

Melody writing is using your imagination to create, express and communicate your idea through sound. When composing, sing the melody out loud or play it on your instrument so you learn how to silently hear the melody in your head. **Composing - Sing It, Play It and Listen to Silently Hear It in Your Head.**

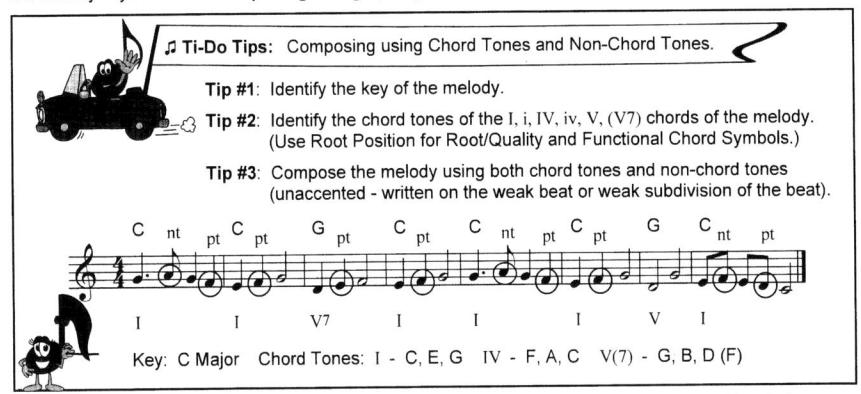

♪ **Ti-Do Tips:** Composing using Chord Tones and Non-Chord Tones.

Tip #1: Identify the key of the melody.

Tip #2: Identify the chord tones of the I, i, IV, iv, V, (V7) chords of the melody. (Use Root Position for Root/Quality and Functional Chord Symbols.)

Tip #3: Compose the melody using both chord tones and non-chord tones (unaccented - written on the weak beat or weak subdivision of the beat).

Key: C Major   Chord Tones: I - C, E, G   IV - F, A, C   V(7) - G, B, D (F)

1. For each of the following melodies: a) Name the key. b) Observe the Functional Chord Symbols to complete each phrase. Use one or more (unaccented) non-chord tones in each melody. c) Circle and label the non-chord tones as "pt" or "nt". d) Write the Root/Quality Chord Symbols above each measure. (one possible answer for each below)

i) Key: C Major

ii) Key: d minor

iii) Key: D Major

iv) Key: a minor

UltimateMusicTheory.com © Copyright 2017 Gloryland Publishing. All Rights Reserved.

COMPOSING - CONTRASTING PERIOD

You're a Composer! There are many exciting ways to explore new sounds and experiment with playing your composition on different instruments, singing your melody or writing it down and hearing it in your head.

So-La Says: Review Composition in the UMT LEVEL 5 & LEVEL 6 Supplemental Workbooks: Parallel and Contrasting Periods. Antecedent - Question Phrase, Consequent - Answer Phrase.

Parallel Period - 2 four-measure phrases: Question "a" (mm. 1 - 4) and Answer "a1" (mm. 5 - 8). Phrase "a" and "a1" begin with parallel (same) melodic material to create similar phrases.

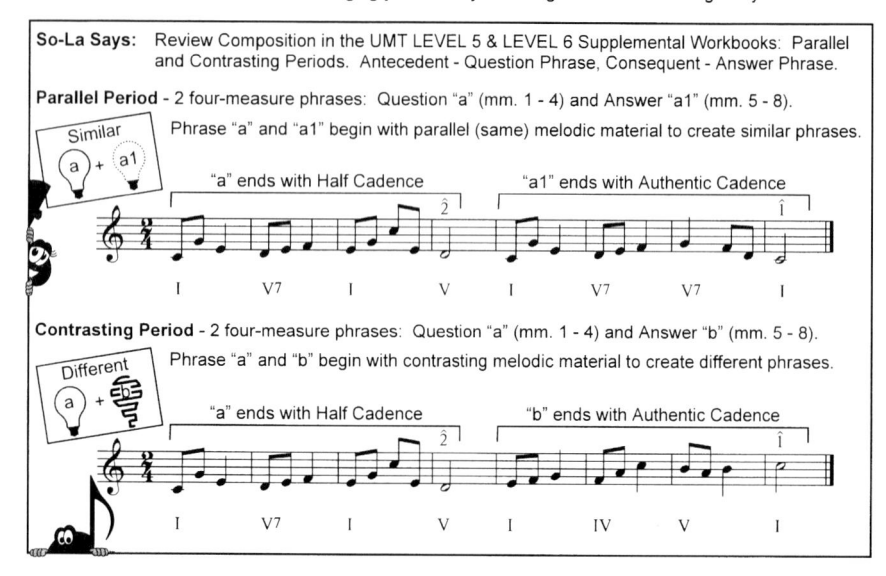

"a" ends with Half Cadence — "a1" ends with Authentic Cadence

I V7 I V I V7 V7 I

Contrasting Period - 2 four-measure phrases: Question "a" (mm. 1 - 4) and Answer "b" (mm. 5 - 8). Phrase "a" and "b" begin with contrasting melodic material to create different phrases.

"a" ends with Half Cadence — "b" ends with Authentic Cadence

I V7 I V I IV V I

♪ **Ti-Do Tip:** In a Contrasting Period, the new contrasting melodic material "b" may use a different rhythm, melody and/or harmonic chord progression. End "b" on the Tonic, stable scale degree $\hat{1}$.

1. Name the key. Compose 2 different Answer Phrases ("b") for the given Question Phrase ("a") to create a Contrasting Period. End on stable scale degree $\hat{1}$. Write Functional Chord Symbols below each measure.
(example answers below)

"a": C (I) — G (V) — C (I) — G (V)

Key: C Major

"b": C (I) — F (IV) — C (I) — G (V) — C (I)

"b": C (I) — F (IV) — G7 (V7) — C (I)

COMPOSING - CONTRASTING PERIOD and CONSEQUENT PHRASES

In a **Contrasting Period**, when composing a **Consequent "Answer" Phrase** to an Antecedent "Question" Phrase, use the KISS Method - "*Keep It Super Simple*".

♪ **Ti-Do Tips:** *Keep It Super Simple* when writing an Answer Phrase to create a Contrasting Period.

Tip #1: Use melodic and rhythmic ideas from the Question phrase, with a few changes. Reflect the character of the Question in the Answer Phrase.

Tip #2: Do not use too many new ideas or too many "busy" notes in your Answer Phrase.

Tip #3: Use mostly stepwise motion, skips and short leaps (interval of a 4th or 5th).

Tip #4: The Leading Tone moves to the Tonic or another note of the Dominant chord. Remember to raise the 7th note (Leading Tone) in a minor key.

Tip #5: Move by step to end on the Tonic note on the first Basic Beat of the last measure (long note value). Sing or play your composition. Add So-La Sparkles!

1. For each of the following: a) Name the key. b) Compose an Answer Phrase for the given Question Phrase to create a Contrasting Period. c) Draw a phrase mark over each phrase (use square phrases). d) Name the type of cadence (Authentic or Half) directly below each phrase ending.

COMPOSING - CONTRASTING PERIOD - MELODIC STRUCTURE

A Melody has a **Melodic Structure** of tones that have a relationship to one another. The characteristics of a melody are: **Range** - narrow, medium or wide (lowest to highest pitch); **Shape or curve** - conjunct (step), disjunct (skip or leap) or stasis (repeat) and **Direction** - movement (up or down).

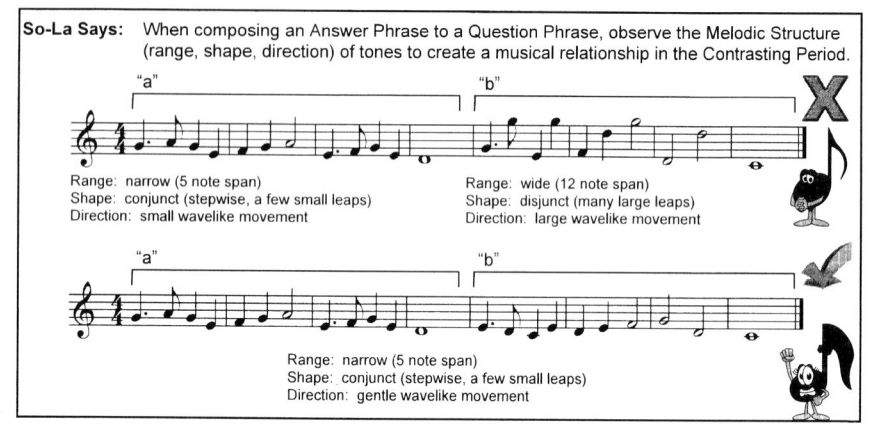

So-La Says: When composing an Answer Phrase to a Question Phrase, observe the Melodic Structure (range, shape, direction) of tones to create a musical relationship in the Contrasting Period.

"a"
"b"

Range: narrow (5 note span)
Shape: conjunct (stepwise, a few small leaps)
Direction: small wavelike movement

Range: wide (12 note span)
Shape: disjunct (many large leaps)
Direction: large wavelike movement

"a"
"b"

Range: narrow (5 note span)
Shape: conjunct (stepwise, a few small leaps)
Direction: gentle wavelike movement

1. For each of the following: a) Name the key. b) Compose an Answer Phrase for the given Question Phrase to create a Contrasting Period. c) Draw a phrase mark over each phrase (use square phrases). d) Name the type of cadence (Authentic or Half) directly below each phrase ending.

(one possible answer for each below)

i) Key: E♭ Major   Cadence: Half
   Cadence: Authentic

ii) Key: F Major   Cadence: Half
    Cadence: Authentic

COMPOSING - CONTRASTING PERIOD - RHYTHMIC STRUCTURE

A Melody has a **Rhythmic Structure** of values that have a relationship to one another. The characteristics of rhythm are: **Duration** - sound/silence (length of note/rest value); **Pattern** - pulse (strong, weak, medium) and **Flow** - controlled movement of the rhythmic patterns. Composition has Rhythmic and Melodic Structure.

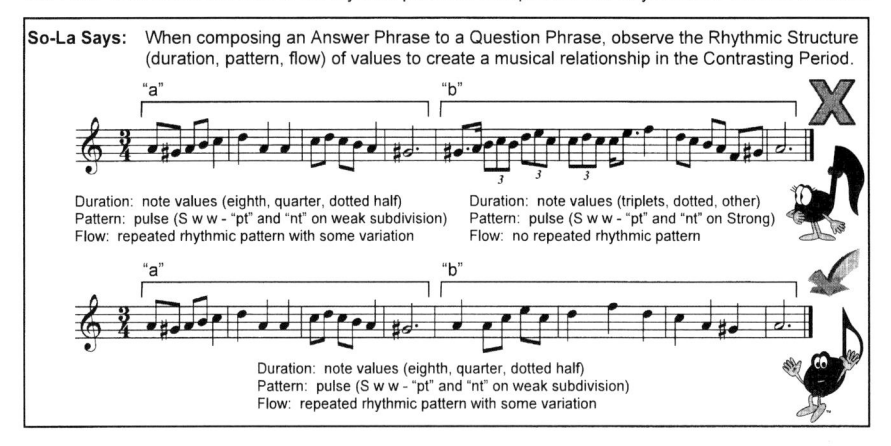

So-La Says: When composing an Answer Phrase to a Question Phrase, observe the Rhythmic Structure (duration, pattern, flow) of values to create a musical relationship in the Contrasting Period.

"a"
"b"

Duration: note values (eighth, quarter, dotted half)
Pattern: pulse (S w w - "pt" and "nt" on weak subdivision)
Flow: repeated rhythmic pattern with some variation

Duration: note values (triplets, dotted, other)
Pattern: pulse (S w w - "pt" and "nt" on Strong)
Flow: no repeated rhythmic pattern

"a"
"b"

Duration: note values (eighth, quarter, dotted half)
Pattern: pulse (S w w - "pt" and "nt" on weak subdivision)
Flow: repeated rhythmic pattern with some variation

1. For each of the following: a) Name the key. b) Compose an Answer Phrase for the given Question Phrase to create a Contrasting Period. c) Draw a phrase mark over each phrase (use square phrases). d) Name the type of cadence (Authentic or Half) directly below each phrase ending.

(one possible answer for each below)

i) Key: **G Major** I V7 V7 I I IV I V Cadence: **Half**

I IV I V V7 I Cadence: **Authentic**

ii) Key: **C Major** I V7 I V Cadence: **Half**

I IV I V7 I Cadence: **Authentic**

FORM and ANALYSIS - IDENTIFICATION of HARMONIC PROGRESSIONS

The Melodic and Rhythmic Structure of a melody is built on a **Harmonic Progression**. A Harmonic Progression refers to the order of chords used in the music or implied by the melody.

So-La Says: The chords in a Harmonic Progression can be identified using Root/Quality Chord Symbols or Functional Chord Symbols. Major or minors chords (I, i, IV, iv, V, V7) of a progression are implied by the notes of the melody and the accompaniment.

A Melody may contain chord tones from the Harmonic Progression or unaccented non-chord tones ("pt" or "nt") to embellish the melodic line, adding interest and variety to the music. The same harmonic chord progressions may be used with different melodic lines.

1. Analyze each of the following melodies to identify the Harmonic Progression. a) Name the key.
   b) Write the Functional Chord Symbols (root position only) for the implied Harmonic Progression directly below each measure. c) Label the cadence at the end of each phrase as Authentic or Half.

i) Functional Chord Symbol: I V^7 I V I V^7 I V I
   Key: F Major   Cadence: Half   Cadence: Authentic

ii) Functional Chord Symbol: i V^7 i V i iv V i
    Key: a minor   Cadence: Half   Cadence: Authentic

iii) Functional Chord Symbol: I IV I V I IV V^7 I
     Key: C Major   Cadence: Half   Cadence: Authentic

FORM and ANALYSIS - HARMONIC PROGRESSIONS and HARMONIC RHYTHM

Harmonic Progression is a series of different chords written one after the other. A Cadence is a two Chord Progression: Authentic Cadence (final cadence ends on I, i), Half Cadence (non-final cadence ends on V).

Harmonic Rhythm is the speed at which chords change in a **Harmonic Progression**. Harmonic Rhythm (harmonic tempo) is determined by the melodic line and the Time Signature. The harmonic rhythm often slows down at the end of a phrase, ending with a final or non-final cadence.

> **So-La Says:** Harmonic Rhythm greatly affects the mood & style of the music by the speed & regularity of chord changes. Regular harmonic rhythm creates a feeling of comfort, stability, balance & forward momentum. Irregular harmonic rhythm creates a feeling of discomfort & distress.
>
> Harmonic Rhythm usual chord changes are: **Duple meter** - Beat 1 or Beats 1 & 2; **Triple meter** - Beat 1 or Beats 1 & 3; **Quadruple meter** - Beat 1 or Beats 1 & 4, Beats 1 & 3 or Beats 1, 2, 3, 4. Fast moving music has slow harmonic rhythm. Slow moving music has fast harmonic rhythm.

♪ **Ti-Do Tip:** Creating a Chord Chart (either on your Whiteboard or in the margin before the music) makes identifying Chord Tones (the notes in each Chord) and non-chord tones (pt/nt) easy.

1. For each melody: a) Name the key. Complete the Chord Chart with the Chord Tones. b) Following the Harmonic Rhythm, write the Root/Quality Chord Symbol above and the Functional Chord Symbol below. c) Circle and label any non-chord tones.

IMAGINE, COMPOSE, EXPLORE

♪ Imagine - Use your imagination to create a title that describes your composition.
♪ Compose - Write your composition and add your name (top right) as the composer.
♪ Explore - Add "So-La Sparkles" (terms & signs) to express how the music is played.

So-La Says: **When composing follow these 3 Composing Steps:**

1. Record your melody as you play. Use it as a reference.
2. Write your melody on the Whiteboard. Try different ideas.
3. Write your melody in the workbook. Add "So-La Sparkles" of articulation, dynamics, etc. to create your final composition.

1. Complete the following melody to create a Contrasting Period. Add a title and your name (composer).
    a) Name the key. Add the correct Time Signature directly below the bracket.
    b) Complete the first Question phrase ending on an unstable scale degree. Label the degree number.
    c) Compose the Answer phrase ending on a stable scale degree. Label the degree number.
    d) Add Functional Chord Symbols below each measure as needed. Add "So-La Sparkles" and Play!
    (one possible answer below)

The Day I Forgot To Do The Thing I Was Supposed To Do But Didn't Because…

My Dog Jumped Into The Garden
(title)

Miss Sassy
(composer)

Vivo ed scherzando

V I p V⁷   I   V mf

Key: G Major

I   IV   dim.   I   V⁷   I

♫ Ti-Do Time: Get your "Composers Certificate". SCAN your composition (on this page) and send it to us at: info@ultimatemusictheory.com and we will send you a special **Ultimate Music Theory Composers Certificate** - FREE.

ANALYSIS and SIGHT READING

Forest Frog
Julianne Warkentin

Vivo ed giocoso

[Sheet music with labeled boxes A, B, C, D, E, F, G and measure number boxes 4 and 7]

1. Analyze the music by answering the questions below. Play (Sight Read) the piece "Forest Frog".

   a) Add the correct Time Signature directly below the bracket. Name the key: __e minor__

   b) Explain the term *Vivo ed giocoso*. __lively and humorous__

   c) Name the interval at letter A: __dim 5__   Name both notes, lower note first: __E__ __B♭__

   d) At letter B, identify the chord: Root: __C__ Type/Quality: __Dom 7th__ Position: __root pos__

   e) At letter C, identify the chord note names: lower note first __C D♯ F♯ A__ Type/Quality: __dim 7th__

   f) Name the interval at letter D: __dim 4__   Name both notes, lower note first: __D♯__ __G__

   g) Name the interval at letter E: __min 3__   Name both notes, lower note first: __D♯__ __F♯__

   h) At letter F, identify the chord: Root: __E__ Type/Quality: __minor__ Position: __root pos__

   i) Write the measure number in the box directly above line 2 & 3. Total number of measures: __9__

   j) Name and explain the sign at letter G: __fermata - hold note longer than written__
      __(pause)__   __value__

MUSIC HISTORY - ROMANTIC ERA (1825 - 1900) AND FELIX MENDELSSOHN

In the **Romantic Era**, the Spirit of Romanticism expressed personal feelings, imaginative ideas and views of the world through freedom of expression in music, poetry and art. Romantic Composers such as Brahms, Tchaikovsky and **Felix Mendelssohn** used descriptive titles and virtuoso passages to express emotion.

German composer Felix Mendelssohn-Bartholdy (1809 - 1847) was a musical prodigy born into a wealthy prominent family. He began performing and composing at an early age.

Mendelssohn's creativity was expressed through his music as well as reflected through his paintings and drawings.

"The essence of the beautiful is unity in variety."
~ Felix Mendelssohn

Mendelssohn was an educator, musician, conductor and composer of piano music (*Songs without Words*), concertos (violin and piano), operas, symphonies, sonatas (viola, clarinet, violin), string quartets and more.

Felix Mendelssohn's older sister Fanny Mendelssohn (1805 - 1847) was a pianist and composer who wrote over 400 pieces, including short lyrical piano pieces (*Songs without Words - Lieder ohne Worte*). Some of her works were originally published under her brother Felix Mendelssohn's name.

Felix and Fanny, both musical prodigies, played music together and put on plays together including Shakespeare's comedy *A Midsummer Night's Dream*.

Felix Mendelssohn wrote the Concert Overture to *A Midsummer Night's Dream* when he was 17 years old, using the Classical Sonata Form. It was originally written as a piano duet (performed with his sister Fanny).

Program Music is instrumental music which is given a descriptive title (based on a literary program or pictorial associations), designed to evoke (suggest or create) extra-musical ideas or images for the listener.

Concert Overture is a single-movement concert piece for orchestra. (A type of Program Music, it tells a story or describes a scene.) It may use the Classical Sonata Form or the Free Form of a Symphonic Poem.

Sonata Form is a one movement instrumental work with a distinct 3 section structure of: Exposition, Development and Recapitulation. Musical Themes (or Subjects) are developed and explored.

Free Form of a Symphonic Poem (Tone Poem) is a one-movement orchestral form which freely illustrates a poetic idea, scene, painting or other non-musical source to inspire the imagination of its listeners.

Go to **GSGMUSIC.com** - For Easy Access to listening to Mendelssohn's *A Midsummer Night's Dream*.

1. The Musical Period (1825 - 1900) of Felix Mendelssohn is called the **Romantic Era**.
2. The Form Felix Mendelssohn used in *A Midsummer Night's Dream* is called **Sonata Form**.
3. The Spirit of Romanticism expressed **personal feelings, imaginative ideas**.
4. Instrumental music with a descriptive title based on a literary idea is called **Program Music**.
5. A single-movement concert piece for orchestra is called **Concert Overture**.
6. **Sonata** Form has Three Sections: Exposition, Development and Recapitulation.
7. A one-movement form freely illustrating a poetic idea, scene, painting is a **Symphonic** Poem.

MUSIC HISTORY - MENDELSSOHN - OVERTURE TO A MIDSUMMER NIGHT'S DREAM

Mendelssohn's Overture to *A Midsummer Night's Dream* in E Major is in the Genre of Concert Overture, for Performing Forces of a symphony orchestra. William Shakespeare's play, *A Midsummer Night's Dream*, is a magical comedy about hilarious woodland fairies in an enchanted forest who fumble (mix things up) as they clumsily try to control the love lives of ordinary people.

Mendelssohn's Overture was not written to be performed with Shakespeare's play. Instead, Mendelssohn selected important elements of drama from the entire play to use in his Romantic Period Concert Overture (storytelling/describing a scene), structured as a one movement symphonic work in Classical Sonata Form.

Exposition - Statement of contrasting themes 1, 2a, 2b. Development - Departure as theme 1 is developed. Recapitulation - Return of the exposition themes. The overture begins with a 5 measure Introduction.

Introduction mm. 1 - 5 Four "magic" chords played by woodwind and brass. The texture thickens as each measure introduces an instrument with a unique timbre to build drama (as if to cast a spell, transporting us into the enchanted forest where King Oberon and Queen Titania rule the Fairy Kingdom).

M. 1 - Two flutes begin in m. 1, playing E and G#, indicating two possible keys: E Major or c# minor.

M. 2 - Clarinets are added in m. 2, playing B Major chord (B D# F#), indicating the V chord of E Major.

M. 3 - Bassoons and horns are added in m. 3, playing a minor chord (A C E) indicating the iv chord, a modal shift from Major to minor (the first shift of many to follow).

M. 4 - Oboes are added in m. 4, playing the final chord I, indicating the Tonic key of E Major. The Plagal Progression (I, V, iv, I) may suggest the rise and fall of the curtains on this drama of enchantment.

MM. 1 - 5 - A *fermata* above each of the 4 chords suggests that the tempo of *Allegro di molto* actually doesn't begin until m. 6, setting the mood for the fairy music that follows. "Magic".

Go to **GSGMUSIC.com** - For Easy Access to see the full musical score while listening to the music. Watch the symphony orchestra perform the Overture to *A Midsummer Night's Dream*.

1. The composer of the Overture to *A Midsummer Night's Dream* is __Felix Mendelssohn__.
2. The Overture to *A Midsummer Night's Dream* was based on the play by __Shakespeare__.
3. This Overture is written for Performing Forces of a __symphony orchestra__.
4. In the introduction, as each measure introduces an instrument, the __texture__ thickens.
5. The sound of each instrument builds drama and adds a new tone color with its unique __timbre__.
6. This piece is in the key of __E Major__. The iv chord in measure 3 is a modal shift to __e minor__.
7. The *Allegro di molto* tempo is altered with sustained notes indicated by __fermata__ signs.

MENDELSSOHN - OVERTURE TO A MIDSUMMER NIGHT'S DREAM - EXPOSITION

A Midsummer Night's Dream in E Major is scored for 2 flutes, 2 oboes, 2 clarinets, 2 bassoons, 2 horns, 2 trumpets, ophicleide (keyed bass brass 'bugle' instrument with a cup mouthpiece), timpani and strings.

Musical elements (dynamics, tempo, texture) and timbre of the instruments are used to create sounds and images of characters in our imagination, such as string instruments creating dancing woodland fairies.

Exposition mm. 6 - 249 (Keys: e minor, E Major); Three contrasting themes - Three contrasting characters.

Theme 1 mm. 6 - 61 (e minor) the Fairies. The String Section links the introduction to Theme 1, playing a sustained chord in the unexpected key of e minor (Tonic minor of E Major) to call the dancing fairies.

Shakespeare's fairies, rushing through the forest with fluttering wings, are characterized by light, rapid eighth note movements with staccato high pitched notes played by violins and pizzicato played by violas.

Transition mm. 62 - 129 (E Major) the Royal Court of Theseus, Duke of Athens. The orchestra establishes the Tonic key of E Major with a sudden fortissimo. The ophicleide is heard for the first time. Theseus' theme uses augmentation, imitation and modulation to move into the Dominant key of B Major.

Theme 2a mm. 130 - 193 (B Major) the two pairs of lovers discover their complicated relationships. The music becomes legato and piano. The soft lyrical melody is played by the 1st violins from measure 138.

Theme 2b mm. 194 - 222 the Rustics (Mechanicals) rehearsing to perform a play for Theseus. One of the Rustics, Nick Bottom (a weaver, comic and stubborn character in the play), is transformed into a donkey.

Mendelssohn uses a repeated dissonant interval of a descending 9th (all instruments playing the same rhythm), which clearly indicates the donkey braying "hee haw".

Go to **GSGMUSIC.com** - For Easy Access to videos about the ophicleide and *A Midsummer Night's Dream*.

1. Theme 1 characterizes the fluttering wings of fairies with a rhythm of light and rapid _eighth_ notes.
2. Theme 1 characterizes the fairies using: dynamics _pp_, key _e minor_, articulation _staccato_.
3. The Transition establishes the Tonic key of _E Major_ and moves to the Dominant key of _B Major_.
4. Theme 2a describes two pairs of lovers using: dynamics _p_, key _B Major_, articulation _legato_.
5. Theme 2b describes Nick Bottom, a comical character who is transformed into a _donkey_.
6. To describe "Bottom's" transformed character, Mendelssohn uses intervals of a descending _9th_.

OVERTURE TO A MIDSUMMER NIGHT'S DREAM - DEVELOPMENT & RECAPITULATION

The **Codetta** mm. 222 - 249 (concluding section of the Exposition) begins with "hunting calls" in horns and trumpets (the royal hunting party of Theseus, who is engaged to Hippolyta, Queen of the Amazons). With all the character themes having been introduced, the stage is set for all the interactions of the characters in the forest setting.

Development mm. 250 - 393 is based mainly on the Fairy Theme 1. The section begins with a sudden key change as Theme 1 is played in b minor (Tonic minor of B Major) and develops in various keys including f sharp minor, e minor, b minor and D Major. Part of the love Theme 2a returns quietly, slowing down. The Development Section ends with a repeated chord in c sharp minor (relative minor of E Major).

Recapitulation mm. 394 - 619 the Four "magic" chords from the introduction return in c sharp minor. The Fairy Theme 1 returns in a shorter form. Theme 2a returns in the Tonic key (E Major).

The recapitulation peaks our imagination with a timpani roll on the Tonic key, the transition theme of the Royal Music of the Court of Theseus, hunting music followed by all playing the Tonic Chord of E major suggesting that the music has come to an end.

Coda mm. 620 - 686 the final surprise, the Fairy Theme is heard again in e minor. The Overture ends as it began with Four "magic" chords, ending with a dream-like quality of a dominant timpani roll on the final chord in E Major. The characters leave the forest believing this was a midsummer nights' dream.

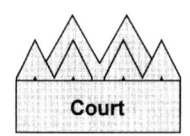

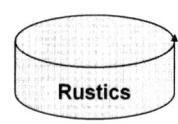

Fairies | **Court** | **Lovers** | **Rustics**

1. In the Introduction, the "magic" chords are played by the __Woodwind__ and __brass__.
2. In the Exposition, Theme 1 describes the characters of the dancing woodland __Fairies__.
3. In the Transition, the opicleide is heard in the Royal __Court__ of Theseus, Duke of Athens.
4. In the Theme 2a, the soft lyrical melody in B Major describes the two pairs of __Lovers__.
5. In the Theme 2b, the donkey hee haw represents the transformed Bottom, one of the __Rustics__.
6. In the Development Section, the main theme that is developed in various keys is __Fairy Theme 1__.
7. In the Recapitulation, the Four "magic" chords return in the key of __C sharp minor__.
8. The Coda ends the Overture in E Major as it began with __Four "Magic" Chords__.

In 1826, Mendelssohn wrote the Concert Overture of *A Midsummer Night's Dream* Op. 21. In 1842, Mendelssohn wrote incidental music to *A Midsummer Night's Dream* Op. 61 (which includes themes from the Overture). This was commissioned by the King of Prussia for a production of Shakespeare's Play.

Play Mendelssohn's "Wedding March" from his suite of incidental music to *A Midsummer Night's Dream*.

MUSIC HISTORY - ROMANTIC ERA (1825 - 1900) AND FREDERIC CHOPIN

In the **Romantic Era**, the piano became a popular instrument and shaped the musical culture. The piano made it possible to play melody and harmony together, which brought the rise of the piano recital. The virtuoso performer, often being the composer (such as Mendelssohn and **Frédéric Chopin**), introduced their own piano concertos to the public. This led to the development of the modern concert grand piano.

> Frédéric Chopin (1810 - 1849) was born in a village near Warsaw, Poland. He was the second child of four and had 3 sisters. His father was French and mother was Polish. He was a child prodigy, highly skilled pianist, teacher & master composer for the piano.
>
> Chopin was reflective, poetic and ultra-sensitive. Known as the "Poet of the Piano" for rich harmonies, lyrical melodies, dashing arpeggios and rhythmic freedom (rubato).
>
> *"Simplicity is the final achievement. After one has played a vast quantity of notes and more notes, it is simplicity that emerges as the crowning reward of art."*
> ~ Frédéric Chopin

At the age of 20, Chopin went to Germany, France and Austria, never to return to Poland. In 1830, the Russians captured Warsaw in a revolutionary uprising. This threw Chopin into a rage. He never forgave Russia and he never played in Russia. Instead, Chopin expressed his devoted love, support and patriotism for Poland through his polonaises, mazurkas and *Étude* Op. 10, No. 12. in C minor (*Revolutionary Étude*).

> **Musical Nationalism** is the use of musical ideas that are identified with a composer's country/region, to show patriotism. Chopin's nationalism evoked the character of Poland's strength, culture and individuality.
>
> **Étude** (French for "study") is a composition for solo instrument written to "study" 1 or 2 specific playing techniques for finger and hand dexterity. Chopin's Concert Etudes were written for the virtuoso performer.
>
> **Rubato** (Italian for "robbed") "Robbed Time" refers to playing a melody, using a flexible tempo, while the underlying pulse remains steady. The slight speeding up and slowing down is an expression of the performer's own emotional input. Chopin's free flowing expressiveness was through exquisite rubato.
>
> **Chromaticism** (Greek for "Colour") is the use of notes not belonging to the key (Key Signature), to add the "color" created by the dissonance of these chromatic notes. Chopin - innovative use of chromatic harmony.

Chopin composed three sets of solo studies for piano. 12 *Études* in Op. 10 (No. 12 the *Revolutionary Étude*), 12 *Études* in Op. 25 and a set of 3 *Études* without an opus number, all with harmonic and structural balance.

Chopin explored the technical resources of the piano in such a way as to provide music of a vast emotional range, music that inspired performers to play with expressive phrasing, beautiful tone, dramatic expression and lyricism, as in his Op. 10, No. 12 in C minor, (nicknamed) the *Revolutionary Étude*.

Go to **GSGMUSIC.com** - For Easy Access to listening to Chopin's Op. 10, No. 12 *"Revolutionary Étude"*.

1. Chopin's *Étude* Op. 10, No. 12 in c minor was nicknamed the __Revolutionary Étude__.
2. The *Étude* Op. 10, No. 12 showed Chopin's Musical __Nationalism__ for Poland.
3. Frédéric Chopin was reflective and poetic and known as the __Poet__ of the __Piano__.
4. Chopin used a rhythmic flexible tempo with free flowing expressiveness called __Rubato__.
5. A composition for solo instrument written to study finger and hand dexterity is called an __Etude__.
6. __Chromaticism__ is using dissonant notes that do not belong to the Key Signature (music).
7. A virtuoso piano piece by Frédéric Chopin is __Etude Op. 10 No. 12 (Revolutionary Étude)__.

MUSIC HISTORY - FREDERIC CHOPIN - *ÉTUDE* Op. 10, No. 12 (REVOLUTIONARY ETUDE)

Frédéric Chopin's *Étude* Op. 10, No. 12 (*Revolutionary Étude*); Key: C minor, Performing Forces: Piano, Genre: solo piano work, Form: Ternary ABA', Tempo: *Allegro con fuoco*, Patriotism: Musical Nationalism.

Ternary Form: **Section A mm. 1 - 28** | **Section B mm. 29 - 40** | **Section A' mm. 41 - 84**
A mm. 1 - 8, 9 - 18, 19 - 28 (introduction + two phrases) | **B** mm. 29 - 32, 33 - 40 (two phrases) | **A'** mm. 41 - 48, mm. 49 - 58, 59 - 68, 69 - 76, 77 - 84 (introduction + three phrases + coda)

Section A mm. 1 - 28 The introduction begins with a crash of the first dramatic chord of indignation (anger provoked by what is perceived as unfair), a Dominant Seventh Chord that creates tension. This is followed by a descending swirl of *legatissimo* (very smooth) sixteenth notes symbolizing resentment and despair.

The left hand rapid sixteenth notes of broken chords, arpeggios and chromatic harmonies create a feeling of turmoil *con fuoco* (with fire). The right hand creates a boldly increasing *appassionato* (passionate, impassioned) with a triumphant rising melody of octaves and chords using dotted rhythmic patterns.

Go to **GSGMUSIC.com** - Free Resources: See the full score and listen to Chopin's *Étude* Op. 10, No. 12.

1. Chopin's *Étude* Op. 10, No. 12 is in the Genre of __Solo piano work__.
2. The Form of Chopin's *Étude* Op. 10, No. 12 is __Ternary Form (ABA')__.
3. Explain the Tempo of *Étude* Op. 10, No. 12. __Allegro con fuoco (Fast with fire)__
4. The Performing Forces of Chopin's *Étude* Op. 10, No. 12 is (are) __piano__.
5. Resentment and despair are created by a swirl of *con fuoco* __sixteenth__ notes.
6. The increasing *appassionato* with a triumphant melody uses __dotted rhythmic__ patterns.
7. *Étude* Op. 10, No. 12 is a study with rapid runs and turns of technical difficulty for the __left__ hand.

MUSIC HISTORY - FREDERIC CHOPIN - *ÉTUDE* Op. 10, No. 12 SECTION B

Frédéric Chopin's *Étude* **Op. 10, No. 12** (*Revolutionary Étude*) written in C minor (often referred to as the "stormiest key" of all) reflected on Poland's failure in its rebellion against Russia. Understanding the sense of conflict and struggle is essential to interpretation and performance of the music as Chopin had intended.

"All this has caused me so much pain. Who could have foreseen it!"
~ Frédéric Chopin

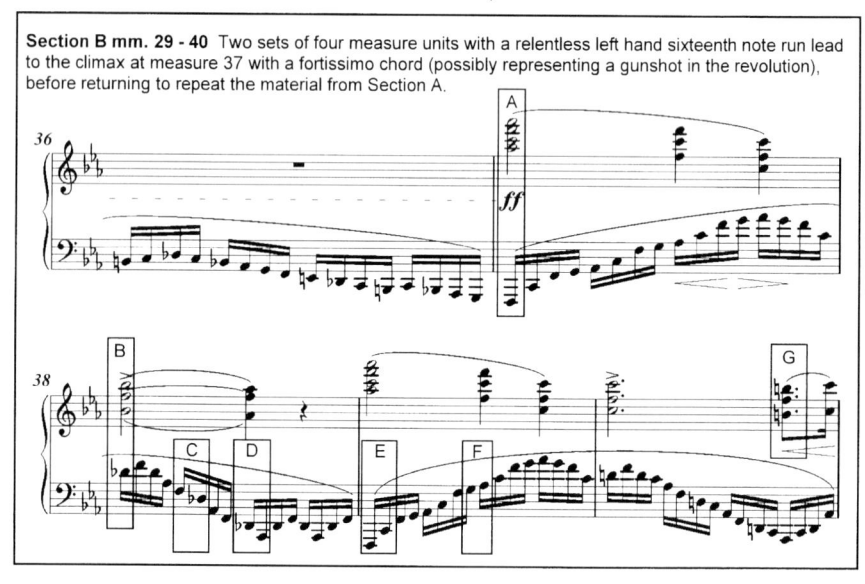

Section B mm. 29 - 40 Two sets of four measure units with a relentless left hand sixteenth note run lead to the climax at measure 37 with a fortissimo chord (possibly representing a gunshot in the revolution), before returning to repeat the material from Section A.

Go to **GSGMUSIC.com** - LEVEL 7 - Listen to *Étude* Op. 10, No. 12. while answering the questions below.

1. In m. 36 of this excerpt, the term for the dissonant notes used is called __Chromaticism__.
2. For the chord at letter A, name the: Root: __F__ Chord Note Names: __F A♭ C__
3. For the chord at letter A, name the: Position: __root pos__ Type/Quality: __minor__
4. For the chord at letter B, name the: Root: __B♭__ Chord Note Names: __B♭ D♭ F__
5. For the chord at letter B, name the: Position: __1st inv__ Type/Quality: __minor__
6. Give the definition for the dynamic term in m. 37. __fortissimo - very loud__
7. Identify the Time Signature. __4/4__ Name the type of note with the largest note value. __dotted halfnote__
8. Name the intervals at: letter C: __Maj 3__, letter D: __Per 4__, letter E: __Per 5__, letter F: __min 2__.
9. Name the type of dotted note at letter G. __dotted eighth note__ The note receives __3/4__ beat(s).
10. *Étude* Op. 10, No. 12, written in C minor is often referred to as the "__stormiest__ key" of all.

MUSIC HISTORY - FREDERIC CHOPIN - *ÉTUDE* Op. 10, No. 12 SECTION A'

Frédéric Chopin's *Étude* Op. 10, No. 12 (*Revolutionary Étude*) in Ternary Form concludes with Section A'. The thunderous left hand and impassioned right hand may be understood as fighting a battle.

A hard struggle ends the piece as dramatically as it began, but now ending in the Tonic chord of C Major rather than the expected key of c minor. We are left to wonder, was it triumph or defeat?

Section B mm. 41 - 84 In the return of Section A material, the music displays polyrhythm, the playing of 2 different rhythms simultaneously. R.H. plays triplet 8ths against L.H. four 16th notes. This conflict of cross-rhythms (3 against 4) conveys a sense of struggle.

Go to **GSGMUSIC.com** - LEVEL 7 - Watch the "MUST SEE" video of the *Étude* Op. 10, No. 12 performed in concert with orchestral accompaniment. This one may surprise you! Answer the questions below.

Conflicting rhythms played simultaneously is called:	
☐ irregular pulse	☑ polyrhythm

The conflict of cross-rhythms (rhythmic pattern that conveys a sense of struggle) in m. 55 is:	
☑ triplet eighth notes against sixteenth notes	☐ quarter note against sixteenth notes

Dramatic changes in dynamics occur between:	
☐ *mp* and *mf*	☑ *p* and *fz*

Chopin's *Étude* Op. 10, No. 12 (*Revolutionary Étude*) ends with a sense of wonder with a Tonic triad of:	
☑ C Major	☐ c minor

MUSIC HISTORY - MODERN ERA (1900 - PRESENT) IGOR STRAVINSKY - PETRUSHKA CHORD

The **Modern Era** brought innovation (new approaches to musical styles), advancement in technology (audio and video listening/recording devices) and originality (new harmonic and melodic ideas) in composition. 20th Century music developed Polyrhythms, Polytonality and Polychords (including the Petrushka Chord).

Modern Era composers include: Debussy (Impressionism), Schönberg (Expressionism), Webern (Serialism) Reich (Minimalism), Duke Ellington (Jazz), Hugh Le Caine (Electronic Music) & **Igor Stravinsky** (Polytonality).

Igor Stravinsky (1882 - 1971) was born near St. Petersburg, Russia, into a well-to-do family. His father was an opera singer (bass) and his mother was a singer and pianist. Stravinsky studied piano from an early age. He was married and had four children.

Stravinsky studied music theory with master composer and mentor Rimsky-Korsakov. He composed music for piano, orchestra and ballet, including The Firebird, Petrushka and The Rite of Spring. His music was innovative, cutting-edge, controversial and bold.

"To listen is an effort, and just to hear is no merit. A duck hears also."
~ Igor Stravinsky

Stravinsky identified himself as an "*Inventor of Music*". He was one of the most influential composers of the 20th Century. He lived in France, Switzerland and in the USA. In 1960, he was inducted into the Hollywood Walk of Fame. In 1983, the *Stravinsky Fountain* in Paris was created with 16 works of sculpture (with spraying water), representing his works. He "broke the rules" of sound with polytonality (Petrushka Chord).

Polytonality is the use of 2 or more keys sounding simultaneously to create dissonance (tension).

Polychord is a combination of 2 or more chords sounding together, creating dissonance (harsh, clashing). Separately, the chords might be consonant (pleasant).

Petrushka Chord is a polychord of C Major and F sharp Major creating a dissonant sound (a tritone apart).

Stravinsky's Ballet *Petrushka* uses the Petruska Chord (a recurring polytonic device) to identify the title character.

In Scene 2, **Petrushka, the puppet clown** (alone in his cold dark room) is characterized by the Petrushka Chord.

The Petrushka Chord

F# Major Chord and C Major Chord together

Second Tableau (Scene 2) mm. 49 - 51

Go to **GSGMUSIC.com** - For Easy Access to listening to Stravinsky's "*Petrushka*" & the Petrushka Chord.

1. Stravinksy wrote music during the musical period (1900 - present) called _Modern_ Era.
2. Stravinsky's first 3 ballets were: _The Firebird_, _Petrushka_, _The Rite of Spring_.
3. The simultaneous sound of two or more keys used to create dissonance is called _Polytonality_.
4. The polychord made famous by Stravinsky is called the _Petrushka Chord_.
5. The dissonant sound between C Major and F sharp Major chord is a distance of a _tritone_ apart.
6. The ballet's main character 'Puppet Clown' (alone in his cold dark room) is named _Petrushka_.
7. Identify the intervals between the following notes: C - F# _Aug 4_, E - A# _Aug 4_, G - C# _Aug 4_.

MUSIC HISTORY - IGOR STRAVINSKY - PETRUSHKA - BALLET

Igor Stravinsky was commissioned to compose the music for the **Ballet - Petrushka** (1911) by impresario Sergei Diaghilev, producer-director and founder of the Ballets Russes Company (1909 - 1929).

The **Genre of Ballet** is non-verbal storytelling through artistic choreography (dance with highly formalized steps using pointe shoes) performed to music, reflecting the costumed characters' actions and emotions.

> The **ballet Petrushka** tells the story of three puppets brought to life by the Old Showman (Magician): the clown **Petrushka**, who falls in love with the **Ballerina** and eventually is killed by the **Moor**. The story is in 4 *Tableax* (scenes), beginning with the **Shrovetide Fair**.
>
> First Tableau: The Shrovetide Fair - A busy crowd at a winter celebration in St. Petersburg, full of colorful performers and carnival rides. The old Showman presents a Puppet Show playing his enchanted flute, casting a spell to bring his 3 puppets to life. Crowds are amazed as the puppets perform a lively Russian folk dance.

Petrushka is nationalistic as Stravinsky includes Russian subjects, folk music and features Russian Dance.

The **Performing Forces** of the Ballet are large orchestra with expanded percussion, including piano.

The Shrovetide Fair is in three parts. Part One: *"The Crowd Revels at the Shrovetide Fair"*, Part Two: *"The Arrival of the Showman"*, Part Three: *"The Puppets Come to Life"*.

First Tableau - Part One: *"The Crowd Revels at the Shrovetide Fair"*, tempo *Vivace*, is in **Rondo Form**. Three alternating principle themes A, B and C create the Classical Rondo Form - ABACABA.

> Section A: Crowd Scene, Section B: Song of the Drunken Beggars, Section A: Returns - modified, Section C: Hurdy-Gurdy Player, followed by the return of Sections A, B, A.

Go to **GSGMUSIC.com** - Free Resources - Watch the ballet *Petrushka* First Tableau: The Shrovetide Fair.

1. Listen to Stravinsky's Petrushka, First Tableau - Part One. Check (✓) the correct answer below.

The Form of Stravinsky's Petrushka, First Tableau - Part One is:
☐ sonata form ☑ rondo form ☐ ternary form

The Genre of Stravinsky's Petrushka is:
☑ ballet ☐ concert overture ☐ electronic music

The themes of Stravinsky's Petrushka, First Tableau - Part One are presented as:
☐ ABCAB ☐ ABACA ☑ ABACABA

The Performing Forces of Stravinsky's Petrushka is:
☐ large orchestra with full choir (SATB) ☐ string quartet with 2 double bass ☑ large orchestra with expanded percussion, including piano

MUSIC HISTORY - IGOR STRAVINSKY - PETRUSHKA BALLET - SECTION A and SECTION B

Stravinsky's Petrushka First Tableau - Part One: *"The Crowd Revels at the Shrovetide Fair"*, Analysis: Key: D minor, F Major and B flat Major, Tempo: Vivace, Time Signature: 3/4, Form: Rondo (ABACABA).

Section A: Crowd Scene - People on the street at the colorful Shrovetide Fair, coming and going in different directions (distinctly different in tonality and rhythmic pacing). The festive carnival is reflected through changing meters, accents, syncopation (irregular rhythmic accented weak beat) and the high sound of the flute announcing the pentatonic melody (based on the 5 notes of the pentatonic scale).

---

1. Analyze the Section A excerpt from First Tableau - Part One, by answering the questions below.

a) At letter A, identify the term for the irregular rhythmic accented weak beat. __Syncopation__

b) At letter B, name the notes from the pentatonic scale used in the melody. __A, G, E, D, A__

c) At letter C, name the note: __D__   Give the combined value of the tied notes. __1 3/4 beats__

Section B: Song of the Drunken Beggars - A group of drunken merrymakers, dancing and enjoying themselves in a lively and noisy way. The piece features the Russian folk song "Song of the Volochebniki" (Drunken Beggars) with full orchestra. A narrower ranged melody is clearly heard through homophonic chordal texture (melody and accompaniment) and homorhythmic texture (very similar rhythm in all parts).

---

2. Analyze the Section B excerpt from First Tableau - Part One, by answering the questions below.

a) Explain the meaning of the dynamic sign. __very very loud (fortississimo)__

b) The descending five-note pattern at letter A is repeated. Draw a square around each repeated pattern.

c) Circle if the Time Signature for Section A and Section B are the: same   or   **different**.

Section A: Overlapping Section B in returning to Section A creates polytonality. Section A returns the Time Signature to 3/4 Time. Changes in orchestration with brass interruptions adds variety to **A'**.

MUSIC HISTORY - IGOR STRAVINSKY - PETRUSHKA BALLET - SECTION C

Stravinsky's Petrushka First Tableau - Part One: *"The Crowd Revels at the Shrovetide Fair"*, Analysis of Section C includes two dance tunes with changes in Key, Time Signature and featured instrumentation.

> **Section C: Hurdy-Gurdy Player** - The first dance of the Hurdy-Gurdy Player begins in triple meter. The sound of the hurdy-gurdy is suggested by the clarinets. The Hurdy-Gurdy, known in France as the *vielle a roue ('fiddle with a wheel')*, is a fiddle-shaped stringed instrument with 3 to 6 strings which vibrate by a resined wheel turned by a crank.

1. Analyze the Section C excerpt from First Tableau - Part One, dance #1 by answering the questions below.

    a) Identify the melodic intervals at: letter A: __min 6__ letter B: __Maj 2__ letter C: __Per 1__.

    b) The dance begins in triple meter, then changes to __duple__ meter and then to __triple__ meter.

    c) Explain the signs used: tie: __hold for combined value of the tied notes__ tenuto: __held (sustained)__ phrase: __play legato (smoothly)__.

> **Section C: Hurdy-Gurdy Player** - The second dance of the Hury-Gurdy Player begins in duple meter. This is played by flutes and also uses a celesta. A celesta is a percussion instrument (looks like a piano) with small felt hammers that strike metal bars.
> (Tchaikovsky used the celesta to describe the Sugar Plum Fairy in the Nutcracker Ballet.)

2. Analyze the Section C excerpt from First Tableau - Part One, dance #2 by answering the questions below.

    a) Identify the following for this except: Key: __B♭ Major__ Time Signature: __2/4__ Meter: __duple__

    b) Based on the given Functional Chord Symbols, write the Root/Quality Chord Symbols above m. 3 & m. 4.

    c) Identify the type of cadence created with a I - V chord progression. __Half__ cadence

Section A: Returns A', **Section B:** Returns B' with full orchestra and the final **Section A:** Returns A' with a climax of a percussion drum roll bringing Part One: *"The Crowd Revels at the Shrovetide Fair"* to a dramatic conclusion in preparation for Part Two: "The Arrival of the Showman" followed by Part Three: "The Puppets Come to Life" completing the First Tableau of the ballet Petrushka.

Go to **GSGMUSIC.com** - Free Resources to see the full score while listening to Stravinsky's Petrushka.

MUSIC HISTORY - HUGH LE CAINE - ELECTRONIC MUSIC

Electronic Music is a Genre that may be categorized as any music produced and modified through electronic devices such as tape recorders, synthesizers, digital recording devices and computers. Early electronic inventions include the Telharmonium or Dynamophone, Theremin and Electronic Sackbut.

Telharmonium or Dynamophone: large synthesizer built in New York (1906) invented by Thaddeus Cahill.
Theremin: electronic instrument controlled without physical contact (1928) invented by Léon Theremin.
Electronic Sackbut: voltage controlled synthesizer with electronic tone (1945) invented by Hugh Le Caine.
Innovative inventor **Hugh Le Caine** is credited with creating 22 new electronic musical instruments.

Go to **GSGMUSIC.com** - Free Resources to watch videos and learn more about Electronic Music.

Hugh Le Caine (1914 - 1977) was born in Port Arthur (Thunder Bay), Ontario, Canada. He played the piano, organ, guitar & sang in choirs. From an early age, he began experimenting with musical instruments and electronics and became one of the "heroes" of Electronic Music.

Le Caine, a Canadian scientist, was a pioneer in radar technology, microwave transmission and atomic physics. Le Caine used his knowledge as a physicist and musician to create multi-track tape machines, touch-sensitive keyboards and the first synthesizer called the *"Electronic Sackbut"*. Photo credit: National Research Council Canada

Musique concrète (French for "concrete music"), developed in the 1940's, is a form of experimental electronic music. Natural sounds from the environment (human voice, nature, musical instruments, etc.) were recorded on magnetic tape and then altered to create electronic music. Many of the recorded sounds were unconnected to their original sound, such as a single drip of water being altered to various pitches.

Special Purpose Tape Recorder (the "Multi-track"), invented by Le Caine, was used in his *musique concrète* experiment that led to the composition of Dripsody (1955) "Étude for Variable Speed Recorder". Étude (French for "study"), was the study of sound manipulation (single drip of water) resulting in "Dripsody". The normal rules of 19th century Études (melody, harmony, rhythm, meter, etc.) do not apply to Dripsody.

1. Answer the following questions on Electronic Music. Check (✓) the correct answer below.

Le Caine's first voltage controlled synthesizer with electronic tone and touch-sensitive keyboard is:
☑ Electronic Sackbut   ☐ Theremin   ☐ Telharmonium

The Genre of Le Caine's "Dripsody" (Étude for Variable Speed Recorder) is:
☐ solo piano   ☐ concert overture   ☑ electronic music

A 1940's compositional form of experimental music recorded on magnetic tape and then altered is:
☐ Dynamophone   ☑ Musique concrète   ☐ Étude

Le Caine's multi-track recorder used to compose "Dripsody" is:
☐ Hurdy-gurdy   ☐ Computer   ☑ Special Purpose Tape Recorder

MUSIC HISTORY - HUGH LE CAINE - DRIPSODY (1955)

The **Genre of Electronic Music** is an umbrella term used to label music made with recording devices, computers and/or electronic instruments. Electronic Music, a Genre that has subgenres and sub-subgenres, continues to evolve with new innovations in technology, recording devices, instruments, culture, styles, etc.

"Dripsody" (Étude for Variable Speed Recorder) is a 1 min. 28 sec. composition created from the original tape recording of a single drop of water using the Special Purpose Tape Recorder (monophonic version). By 1957 the Multi-track played 6 tapes simultaneously. Dripsody was reworked into a stereo version.

Le Caine's Dripsody (1955) monophonic version is a piece of musique concrète. He spent one night manipulating the initial "*drip*" drop sound into a variety of pitches and rhythmic patterns by splicing together (editing) the tape recording through various techniques.

Le Caine said he named it Dripsody, *"Because it was written by a drip."*

"What a composer of electronic music needs most is not an understanding of the apparatus, but a new understanding of sound." ~ Huge Le Caine

Dripsody - Le Caine used an eyedropper and a metal wastebasket to record the sound of the water drops. After listening to the recording, he selected one single water drop and spliced it onto a short tape loop. Le Caine then took the sound of the "*single drip*" and altered it through various techniques.

Pentatonic Scale - The pitch of the "drip" was altered by *tape speed* (re-recorded at different speeds). The faster the tape was played, the higher the pitch. This enabled him to create different pitches by *changing the tape speed* to produce a five note Pentatonic scale pattern.

Amplitude - The strength and size of the vibration determines the volume when balancing and controlling the loudness of sound. (Larger vibrations make a louder sound.) By playing the recorded sound backwards, *reversing the direction of the tape*, the volume of the dynamics were reversed.

Ostinato - The persistently repeated ostinato patterns were created using *four different tape loops*. Three different speeds created twelve different loops, not needing to add additional splices.

Arpeggio - The 12 note arpeggio was created by *splicing different pitches together* from different playback speeds of the initial water drop. Only twenty-five splices were used to compose the piece.

Echo Effect - The use of tape delay was used by playing a sound on the recorder while *re-recording* the sound at the same time. An echo-like sound of the new recording had a lower amplitude.

Dripsody - Begins and ends with a *single drop of water*. The drip is altered with variations in rhythm intensity, pitch (glissando sounds), texture and amplitude to create Le Caine's Electronic Music masterpiece.

Performing Forces - electronic, recorded sound of a single drop of water manipulated through multi-track.

Go to **GSGMUSIC.com** - Free Resources, listen to Hugh Le Caine's Dripsody. Answer the questions below.

1. The five note scale pattern produced by changing the tape speed is the __Pentatonic Scale__.
2. Reversing the direction of the tape, reversed the volume of the __dynamics__.
3. Four different tape loops were used to create the persistent repeated patterns called __ostinato__.
4. Splicing different pitches from different playback speeds created the 12 note __arpeggio__.
5. Playing a sound and re-recording the sound at the same time created an __echo__ effect.
6. Dripsody begins and ends with the sound of a __single drop of water__.

MUSIC HISTORY - EDWARD KENNEDY "DUKE" ELLINGTON - JAZZ MUSIC

Jazz Music may be described as a mix of European musical ideas with African-American styles (a fusion of spirituals, blues and ragtime) that separates it linguistically and stylistically from any other forms of music.

The **Genre of Jazz** contains essential elements that make Jazz "*JAZZ*": syncopation, rhythmic pulse (known as swing) and improvisation. Jazz starts with the melody and its supporting harmony and evolves through a creative process using techniques such as: call & response, polyrhythms and "blue notes".

Major musicians and composers influencing the evolution of jazz music include Charlie Parker, Miles Davis, Dizzy Gillespie, Louis Armstrong & **Duke Ellington**, America's greatest jazz composer of the 20th Century.

Edward Kennedy "Duke" Ellington (1899 - 1974), born in Washington, D.C., was a jazz composer, bandleader & pianist. His only son Mercer Kennedy continued the Legacy. Duke's 4 grandchildren: Edward Kennedy II, Paul Mercer, Gaye Sandra & Mercedes.

Duke Ellington played a major role in the development of the Big-Band Era, from the "Cotton Club" of New York to collaborating with Billy Strayhorn on "Take the A Train" to 13 Grammy Awards and the prestigious Presidential Medal of Freedom in 1969.

"It Don't Mean a Thing if it Ain't Got That Swing"
~ Duke Ellington

"It Don't Mean a Thing (If it Ain't Got That Swing)" was composed by Duke Ellington and recorded with jazz legend Louis "Satchmo" Armstrong, born in New Orleans (known as the "birth place") of Jazz). Ellington's New York Orchestra was bigger than the New Orleans band, as heard in his 1940's composition "Ko-Ko".

A musical structure used in jazz from New Orleans, Chicago, New York and across the globe, was the twelve-bar blues (blues changes) based on the I, IV and V chords played in any key. The blues progression has a distinctive form of three four-measure phrases, a standard chord structure and duration.

12 Bar Blues Chord Progression consists of 3 four-measure phrases. One standard progression is:

Go to **GSGMUSIC.com** - Free Resources, listen to Duke Ellington's Big Band. Answer the questions below.

1. The Genre known for its syncopation, swing rhythmic pulse and improvisation is __jazz__.
2. Improvisation evolves through a creative process using techniques such as call & __response__.
3. __Duke Ellington__ is known as America's greatest jazz composer of the 20th Century.
4. Jazz music was based on a chord progression known as the __12 Bar Blues__.
5. The standard Jazz chord progression consists of 3 __four-measure__ phrases.
6. New York's Duke Ellington composed his famous Big Band Jazz piece "Ko-Ko" in the year __1940__.

MUSIC HISTORY - DUKE ELLINGTON - KO-KO

Duke Ellington's Ko-Ko - In 2011, Duke Ellington & his Famous Orchestra were inducted into the Grammy Hall of Fame for the 1940 Victor recording of Ko-Ko, receiving a special Grammy Award given to honor recordings of *"lasting historical or qualitative significance which have made contributions to our cultural heritage."*

The **Genre of Jazz** has many subgenres including the **subgenre Big Band** - a jazz group of ten or more, usually 3 trumpets, 2+ trombones, 4+ saxophones and a "rhythm section" of piano, guitar, bass & drums.

Ko-Ko is in the Genre of Jazz - Big Band - Swing Classic, recorded in Chicago on March 6, 1940.

Performing Forces: Big Band Orchestra. A 15 piece orchestra (*soloists) including Brass: 3 Trumpets, 3 Trombones (*Joe "Tricky Sam" Nanton and *Juan Tizol - Valve Trombone), Reeds: 5 Saxophones and Rhythm Section: Drums, Double Bass (*Jimmy Blanton), Guitar, Piano (*Duke Ellington).

Key: E flat minor. The use of D flats and C flats create a sound of the aeolian mode (natural minor).
Structure: Introduction, 7 Jazz Choruses (Jazz Chorus is a complete 12 bar blues form) and Coda.

Ellington's Ko-Ko features call & response with exchanges that slowly transform to build tension and energy.

Time	Chorus	Bars	12 Bar Blues - The Structure of Ko-Ko
0:00	Intro	8	Opening syncopated swing rhythm, tom-tom, baritone saxophone & trombones.
0:12	1	12	Valve trombone solo playing straight, against syncopated jazz element of saxes.
0:31	2	12	Muted Trombone solo - answered by brass section with a moving bass line.
0:49	3	12	Muted Trombone (mute tighter for different timbre), growing intensity & dynamics.
1:08	4	12	Piano solo - whole-tone scales, dissonant harmonics, complexity in reeds & brass.
1:26	5	12	3 Trumpets in unison - main theme (mutes half open), higher pitch with orchestra.
1:44	6	12	Double bass solo - swing with a walking bass style, against full orchestra.
2:03	7	12	Full ensemble - rich score to produce large ensemble sound.
2:22	Coda	4	Recapitulation of Introduction.

Go to **GSGMUSIC.com** - Free Resources - Listen to Ko-Ko. Check (✓) the correct answer below.

The composer of the 20th Century award winning Jazz Piece called "Ko-Ko":

☐ Mercer Ellington   ☑ Duke Ellington   ☐ Mercedes Ellington

The Genre of Ellington's award winning "Ko-Ko":

☐ Piano Concerto   ☐ Concert Overture   ☑ Jazz (Big Band)

Performing Forces for Ellington's "Ko-Ko":

☑ Big Band Orchestra   ☐ String Quartet   ☐ Orchestra & SATB Choir

---

The Musical Structure of Ellington's "Ko-Ko":

☐ Sonata Allegro   ☑ 12 Bar Blues   ☐ Rondo ABACABA

MUSIC HISTORY - BAROQUE, CLASSICAL, ROMANTIC & MODERN ERAS REVIEW

Music History in the UMT Supplemental Workbook Series (PREP LEVEL and LEVELS 1 - 7).

PREP LEVEL: Medieval Period (around 500 - 1450), Renaissance Period (1450 - 1600), Baroque Period (1600 - 1750), Classical Period (1750 to 1825), Romantic Period (1825 - 1900) & 20th/21st Century Period.

LEVEL 1: Orchestral Instruments, Story Telling Through Sound, Prokofiev (Peter and the Wolf) and Camille Saint-Saëns (Carnival of the Animals).

LEVEL 2: Symphony & Opera, Mozart (Twelve Variations on Ah, Vous Dirai-Je Maman), Concerto, Rondo Form, (Horn Concerto No. 4 in E flat Major).

LEVEL 3: Bach, (Anna Magdalena Notebook), Baroque Dances, Petzod (Menuet in G Major), J.S. Bach (French Suite No. 5 in G Major - Gavotte and Gigue).

LEVEL 4: Orchestra Families & Instruments, Britten (Young Person's Guide to the Orchestra), Tchaikovsky (The Nutcracker - Sugar Plum Fairy and Waltz of the Flowers).

LEVEL 5: Voices in Vocal Music, Relationship between Music & Text, Handel (Hallelujah Chorus from Messiah), Mozart (Queen of the Night - The Magic Flute), Arlen (Over the Rainbow).

LEVEL 6: J.S. Bach (Invention in C Major No. 1), Brandenburg Concertos (Concerto No. 5 First Movement) and Mozart (Eine Kleine Nachtmusik).

LEVEL 7: Mendelssohn, Chopin, Stravinsky, Le Caine, Ellington and their works.

Go to **GSGMUSIC.com** - Free Resources - Videos - Listen to the music of the composer's works to review the Music History section in each UMT Supplemental Workbook. Answer the questions below.

1. Name the main ancestor of the harp from the Medieval Period. _Lyre_
2. Name the 4 main sections of the orchestra. _strings, woodwinds, brass, percussion_
3. In Peter and the Wolf, name the orchestral section that created the sound of Peter. _string_
4. Name the Form of Mozart's Horn Concerto No. 4 in E flat Major Third Mvt. _Rondo Form_
5. Name the texture used in the Gigue from Bach's French Suite No. 5 in G Major. _Polyphonic_
6. Give the number of variations used in Britten's Young Person's Guide to the Orchestra. _13_
7. Name the instrument used to represent Tchaikovsky's *Sugar Plum Fairy* in the Nutcracker. _Celesta_
8. Give the term used for the relationship between words and text in Handel's Messiah. _Word Painting_
9. Name the voice type required to perform Mozart's "Queen of the Night". _Coloratura Soprano_
10. Name the Form of Bach's Brandenburg Concerto No. 5, 1st Mvt. _Ritornello Form_

MUSIC HISTORY - COMPOSERS and THEIR FAMOUS WORKS REVIEW

Composers may compose in various genres or identify with one genre. Their works reflect their own unique style of composition. By studying music history, composers and their works, we learn how their life, style, instruments available to them and the period they lived in is reflected and expressed through their music.

Go to GSGMUSIC.com - Free Resources - Listen to Various Genres of Music. Analyze the Rhythm, Meter, Melody, Harmony, Dynamics, Timbre, Texture, Vocal Ranges and Instruments that create each unique work.

1. Complete the Music History Review Chart below.

Overture to A Midsummer Night's Dream Composer: _Mendelssohn_ Period: _Romantic_
Genre: _Concert Overture_ Form: _(Classical) Sonata Form_
Three sections of the form: _Exposition_, _Development_, _Recapitulation_
Performing Forces: _Symphony orchestra_ Based on a play by: _Shakespeare_

Étude Op. 10, No. 12 (Revolutionary Étude) Composer: _Chopin_ Period: _Romantic_
Genre: _Solo piano work_ Form: _Ternary Form_
This piece evokes _Musical Nationalism_, patriotism expressed through music.
Performing Forces: _piano_ The composer was known as the _Poet_ of the _Piano_.

Petrushka Composer: _Stravinsky_ Period: _Modern_
Genre: _Ballet_ "The Crowd Revels at the Shrovetide Fair" Form: _Rondo Form_
Define the type of chord used called the "Petrushka Chord": _polychord (tritone apart)_
Performing Forces: _large orchestra with expanded percussion including piano_

Dripsody Composer: _Hugh Le Caine_ Period: _Modern_
Genre: _Electronic_ Musique concrète - form of _experimental_ music.
Machine the composer invented, used for Dripsody: _Special Purpose Tape Recorder (multi-track)_
Performing Forces: _electronic, recorded sound of a single drop of water manipulated through multi-track_

Ko-Ko Composer: _Duke Ellington_ Period: _Modern_
Genre: _Jazz - Big Band_ Musical Structure: _12 Bar Blues_
This Genre contains elements of syncopation and rhythmic pulse known as _swing_.
Performing Forces: _Big Band Orchestra_

NAME THAT 7th CHORD!

Name each chord as a Dominant 7th Chord (Dom 7) or as a Leading-Tone Diminished 7th Chord (dim 7).

Ultimate Music Theory
Level 7 Theory Exam

Total Score: ___ / 100

The Ultimate Music Theory™ Rudiments Workbooks, Supplemental Workbooks and Exams prepare students for successful completion of the Royal Conservatory of Music Theory Levels.

1. a) Write the following intervals below each of the given notes.

   dim 8   Maj 6   Per 4   min 7   Aug 5

   b) Invert the above intervals in the same clef. Name the inversions.

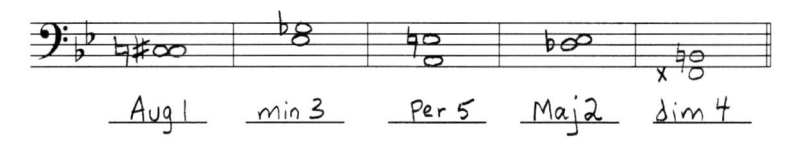

   Aug 1   min 3   Per 5   Maj 2   dim 4

2. a) Write the following triads in the Treble Clef. Use a Key Signature and any necessary accidentals. Use whole notes.

   i) The Dominant Triad of a flat minor, harmonic form, in root position.
   ii) The Mediant Triad of f sharp minor, harmonic form, in second inversion.
   iii) The Submediant Triad of B Major, in first inversion.
   iv) The Supertonic Triad of f minor, harmonic form, in second inversion.
   v) The Subdominant Triad of E Major, in first inversion.

   b) For each of the following seventh chords, name the Major or minor key. Write the Functional Chord Symbol below each chord.

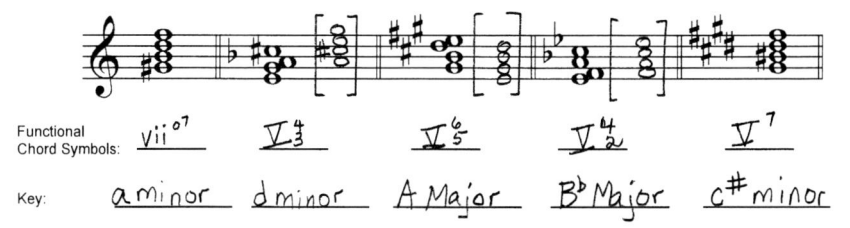

   Functional Chord Symbols: $vii°^7$ V^4_3 V^6_5 V^4_2 V^7

   Key: a minor   d minor   A Major   B♭ Major   c# minor

UltimateMusicTheory.com © Copyright 2017 Gloryland Publishing. All Rights Reserved. 81

Ultimate Music Theory
Level 7 Theory Exam

3. a) Add bar lines to complete each rhythm.

   b) Add the rest(s) below each bracket to complete each measure.

4. For each of the following cadences:
   a) Name the key (Major or minor).
   b) Write the Functional Chord Symbol below each chord and the Root/Quality Chord above.
   c) Name the type of Cadence (Authentic or Half).

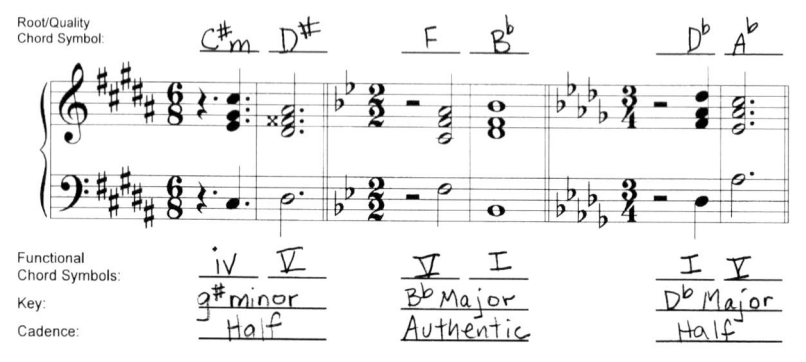

Root/Quality Chord Symbol: C#m   D#   F   Bb   Db   Ab

Functional Chord Symbols: iv V   V   I   I   V
Key: g# minor   Bb Major   Db Major
Cadence: Half   Authentic   Half

UltimateMusicTheory.com © Copyright 2017 Gloryland Publishing. All Rights Reserved. 82

Ultimate Music Theory
Level 7 Theory Exam

5. a) Transpose Measures 1 to 4 (Treble Staff) of Giovanni Platti's Sonata in C Major, Opus 1, No. 2, II Movement down into A♭ Major. Name the Interval of Transposition.

Key: C Major

Interval of Transposition: ↓ Down a Major 3

New Key: A♭ Major

b) Transpose Measures 1 to 4 (Bass Staff) of Giovanni Platti's Sonata in C Major, Opus 1, No. 2, II Movement down a minor 2nd. Name the Original Key and the New Key.

Key: C Major

Interval of Transposition: Down a minor 2nd

New Key: B Major

c) Complete the following Transposition Chart with either the Interval of Transposition or the New Key.

Original Key Name	Interval of Transposition	New Key Name
B Major	Down an Augmented fifth	E♭ Major
c sharp minor	Up a diminished 4	Up to f minor
d minor	Up a minor sixth	b♭ minor
A flat Major	Down diminished 3	Down to F sharp major

UltimateMusicTheory.com © Copyright 2017 Gloryland Publishing. All Rights Reserved.

Ultimate Music Theory
Level 7 Theory Exam

6. Write the following scales, ascending and descending. Use a Key Signature and any necessary accidentals. Use whole notes.

a) The relative Major scale of g minor in the Treble Clef. (B♭ Major)

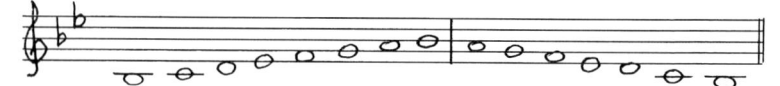

b) Major scale with D as its Submediant in the Bass Clef. (F Major)

c) Chromatic scale starting on C flat in the Bass Clef.

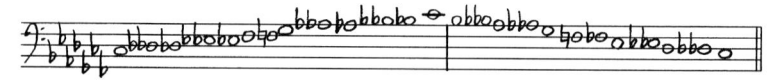

d) The harmonic minor scale with B as the Leading Tone in the Treble Clef. (c minor harmonic)

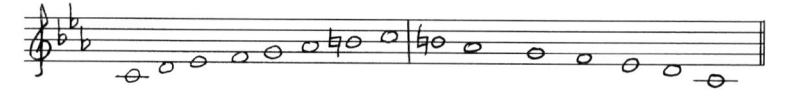

e) The Tonic minor scale (Parallel minor) melodic form of F sharp Major in the Bass Clef. (f# minor melodic)

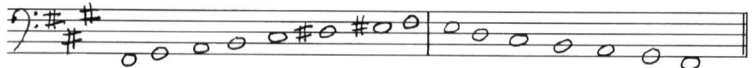

f) Name the following scales as Major Pentatonic, minor Pentatonic, Whole Tone, Blues or Octatonic.

i) Blues

ii) Whole Tone

iii) Octatonic

Ultimate Music Theory
Level 7 Theory Exam

7. a) Name the key of this melody. Write the Time Signature on the music below the bracket.
   b) Compose a four-measure Answer Phrase to create a Contrasting Period ending on a stable scale degree. Label the degree above the note.
   c) Draw a phrase mark over each phrase.
   d) Name the type of each cadence (Authentic or Half) at each phrase ending.

Key: Bb Major   Cadence: Half

(one possible answer)   Cadence: Authentic

e) Name the key of the following melody.
f) Write a cadence in keyboard style at the end of each phrase.
g) Label the cadence chords using Functional Chord Symbols.
h) Name the type of each cadence (Authentic or Half).

V⁷ B D♯ F♯ (A)
IV A C♯ E
I E G♯ B
Chord Chart

Key: E Major

IV   V
Cadence: Half

V   I
Cadence: Authentic

Ultimate Music Theory
Level 7 Theory Exam

8. Identify the work to which each of the following statements applies by writing the appropriate letter (**A**, **B**, **C**, **D** or **E**) in the space before each statement.

___/10

    A - Ko-Ko
    B - Dripsody
    C - Petrushka, First Tableau: "The Crowd Revels at the Shrovetide Fair"
    D - Etude in C minor, Opus 10, No. 12
    E - Overture to A Midsummer Night's Dream

a) __D__ This piece, also known by the name "Revolutionary", was written by Frédéric Chopin.

b) __C__ This ballet features polytonality and a suggested sound of a "Hurdy-Gurdy".

c) __A__ This twelve-bar blues composition features an introduction, 7 choruses and a coda.

d) __C__ Using Russian Folk Songs, this piece demonstrates the composer's nationalism.

e) __B__ The Composer of this piece was also a Canadian Physicist.

f) __B__ This electronic work was written by Hugh Le Caine.

g) __E__ Felix Mendelssohn was inspired by a Shakespeare Play when writing this piece.

h) __C__ This piece was written in Rondo Form by Igor Stravinsky.

i) __B__ This composition was created from the original tape recording of a single drop of water.

j) __A__ This piece is for "Big Band", a subgenre of Jazz, and is performed by a 15 piece orchestra.

9. For each of the following Italian terms, circle TRUE if the definition is true (correct) or circle FALSE if the definition is false (incorrect).

___/10

	True or False			Term	Definition
a)	TRUE	or	**(FALSE)**	tre corde	trio music, music written for three players
b)	**(TRUE)**	or	FALSE	molto agitato	very agitated
c)	**(TRUE)**	or	FALSE	quasi dolente	almost in a sad manner, as if in a sad manner
d)	**(TRUE)**	or	FALSE	poco scherzando	a little playful
e)	TRUE	or	**(FALSE)**	ben marcato	dying, fading away in time and tone
f)	**(TRUE)**	or	FALSE	sotto voce	soft, subdued, under the breath
g)	TRUE	or	**(FALSE)**	quindicesima alta	play two octaves lower
h)	TRUE	or	**(FALSE)**	volti subito, v.s.	second time
i)	TRUE	or	**(FALSE)**	giocoso	grand, grandiose
j)	**(TRUE)**	or	FALSE	martellato	hammered, strongly accented

Ultimate Music Theory
Level 7 Theory Exam

10. Analyze Bach's Minuetto II by answering the questions below.

a) Name the Key. __f minor__ Add the correct Time Signature directly below the bracket.
b) In m. 1, circle and label a non-chord tone as "pt" or "nt". Name the note. __E♮__
c) Name the intervals at: letter A __min 6__, letter B __min 7__, letter C __Maj 2__.
d) Circle if the rhythmic pattern in mm. 1 - 2 and mm. 3 - 4 is: (same) or similar or different.
e) For the chord at letter D, name the: root __A♭__, type/quality __Major__, position __root pos__
f) Circle if the texture of this piece is: monophonic or (homophonic) or polyphonic.
g) Circle if the melodic pattern in mm. 9 - 12 and mm. 13 - 16 is: same or similar or (different).
h) Circle if the scale fragment at letter E is: Major or harmonic minor or (melodic minor).
i) Circle if the Cadence at letter F is: (Authentic) or Half.
j) Label the two sections in this piece as A and B. Name the form of this piece. __Binary__

Ultimate Music Theory Supplemental Answer Books

Bonus - The ONLY Series with identical matching Answer Books!

Top Ten FREE Teacher Resources from Ultimate Music Theory!

#1 **Overview** - Download the UMT Comparison Chart to see each level progression & concepts!

#2 **Lesson Plans** - Detailed concepts with creative teaching tips to save you hours of time!

#3 **Video Lessons** - Teach Basic Rudiments Online Mini-Course including Free eBook!

#4 **Music Theory Worksheets** - Circle of Fifths, staff paper, keyboard pages & much more!

#5 **Music Theory Exams & Answers** - Assess your students easily at every exam level!

#6 **Certificate of Achievement** - Personalize (student's name), print and present for each level!

#7 **100% Club** - Register students when they score 100% on nationally recognized theory exams!

#8 **GSG MUSIC Webinars** - FREE Teacher Training and Professional Development!

#9 **UMT Blog** - Innovative Ideas and Massive Resources for Teaching Music Theory!

#10 **GSG MUSIC Membership & Affiliate Program** - Teacher Training & Business Opportunities!

Questions? (800) 520-4680

UltimateMusicTheory.com

info@ultimatemusictheory.com